Out

in

Front

by Jared Hepler

Out in Front

Jared Hepler

authorHOUSE®

AuthorHouse™ LLC
1663 Liberty Drive
Bloomington, IN 47403
www.authorhouse.com
Phone: 1-800-839-8640

Published by AuthorHouse   11/13/2013

ISBN: 978-1-4918-3049-9 (sc)
ISBN: 978-1-4918-3050-5 (e)

Library of Congress Control Number: 2013920273

*This book is dedicated to my Wife, my Family
and the Service Members and their Families that defend
our Country*

Disclaimers

The names used within these stories have been fabricated to protect the person or persons that the story was written about.

All of the Army Forms that are provided for supporting documentation were provided by the Army Publishing Directorate.

All memorandums provided contain an official Army letter head. This letterhead consists of a Department of Defense Seal and the words "Department of the Army." The DoD nor the Army did not endorse the writing, publication or publishing of this book.

The petition for a restraining order form is an internal form used by the State of Hawaii.

Preface

On June 1st, I stood patiently as the change of command ceremony commenced. Soldiers were formed, the Detachment Sergeant manning his post at the front of his troops as the green guide-on waved behind him, submitting itself to the suggestions of the wind. The guide-on, a green flag embroidered with gold lettering and emblems, represented the Soldiers, the past and things yet to come. K9 teams stood along each side of the path we were to walk down, facing inward with their dog sitting at their side. The stage was set.

The previous Commander, the Battalion Commander and I walked in unison from the audience seating, through the corridor of man and beasts to the formation that stood before us. The commentator begins to describe the tradition of passing the guide-on from the old commander to the new and we coordinated our actions with the words from the speech. The Battalion Commander took the flag from the previous commander's hands and placed it in mine. I had just assumed command of the illustrious 13th Military Police Detachment at Schofield Barracks, Hawaii.

Taking that guide-on from the hands of my Battalion Commander was the beginning of a very rewarding yet extremely challenging road. As I think back to that day, I didn't place as much significance nor took much time to reflect on the enormous responsibility I had just taken on; I had already hit the ground running. The same day I took that flag, I had a Command and Staff meeting to attend, a Special Reaction Team (SRT) that was preparing to go through certification,

Jared Hepler

a kennel that had not passed its annual inspection in over two years and a K9 competition to prepare for; not to mention all the new policy memorandums I had to write and unscrew the debacle of a unit left to me by the previous commander. I had a lot of work to do.

Chapter 1

Leadership is the process of influencing others to accomplish the mission by providing purpose, direction, and motivation.

Throughout my tenure in command, I have seen many challenges. During my time in that seat: I was able to get the Special Reaction Team certified, I was able to weed out the toxic leadership within the Military Working Dog (MWD) kennel section and see the kennel pass its Annual Kennel Inspection and Assessment (AKIA), assumed responsibility for the Soldiers at both Army Police Stations when my sister unit deployed to Afghanistan which doubled the size of my unit, provided countless MWD demonstrations to generals, foreign military's and Hollywood producers, participated as a technical advisor on set as one of my dogs played a part in an episode of the TV series Hawaii 5-0, responded to IG complaints made by spouses claiming that they were not receiving the money that they were owed, had Soldiers get arrested, dealt with all the headaches from the Directorate of Emergency Services (the civilian federal police officers) and their unreliable personnel, fought off a micro-managing senior officer and made it through the transition of the kennel breaking off and becoming their own detachment, which still fell under my command. This would be a very long book if I elaborated on each small stanza that I just wrote and would take away from the overall purpose.

Although tedious and unrelenting, all of the above challenges I felt I was trained for. The Captains Career Course, my time as a Platoon Leader and all the guidance from my superiors and the counsel of some higher enlisted Soldiers prepared me for this job. I was able to get through all of the above with relative ease and was confident I could handle each situation.

That brings me to the point of this literature; the stories contained within these pages, listed in no particular chronological order, are tales of situations I wasn't quite prepared for. Each situation changed me in some way and helped develop me as a leader and a man. There is no Army course that can prepare someone for the unique situations that I was presented with. I had: one senior NCO key his own Soldier's car, one Soldier married to two women at one time, five congressional inquiries initiated on either me or my unit, a female Soldier get beat up by her husband yet still opted to stay with him, a drug addict, a few Soldiers sleeping with spouses that weren't theirs, and the list goes on. In each story, I discuss the events that transpired and what I or SFC Wogomon and I did to resolve it. The names of the Soldiers within the stories have been changed to protect them but their stories are unfortunately true. I encourage you, as a reader, to consider each story and apply critical thinking to each situation. This book isn't meant to portray my actions in each case as the best course of action, it is simply how I handled it, what I thought was legal, moral and ethical. If you would have handled it a different way, that's ok. The purpose of this book is to get you thinking, to help better prepare you for taking on leadership positions and force you to reflect on how you might handle certain issues. This book is not just meant for officers in the military; young Sergeant's, corporate managers and executives, federal agency supervisors and managers, anyone wanting to step into a leadership role at some point in your life; this book's for you.

The Army is an amazing organization that is comprised of hard working and dedicated professionals who stand ready to deploy, engage and destroy the enemies of the United States in close combat. Unfortunately, there are also Soldiers that do not display the values in which we would expect them to exhibit. Most of the stories within these pages describe Soldiers that have faltered from these values and the consequences that followed. This book is not meant to take away from the outstanding men and women within our ranks nor portray the Army as a negative organization, we just have a few exceptions that we either need to remove from our ranks or adjust their behavior. As a leader, it's up to you to help shape the future of your organization.

As you pursue your leadership roles, there are many resources and references you can utilize as you deliberate on what decision to make or what course of action you should take in your own unique situations that I know you will face. Some Army resources you can reference are:

Army Regulation (AR) 600-20—Army Command Policy
AR 600-100—Army Leadership
Field Manual (FM) 6-22—Army Leadership
ADRP 6-22—Army Leadership
ADP 6-22—Army Leadership
The Army Training and Leader Development Process
The Leadership Requirements Model

Although these are Army manuals or publications, the content within them is universal as it pertains to leadership. Your organization or institution should also have publications that will provide you with some insight on leadership that you can research. All of the above resources can be found online for free.

My hope is that my experiences energize your critical thinking capabilities and develop or strengthen your core values that make you who you are. These values will echo through your tenure as a leader and will have an impact on those you are responsible for and their families. Whether it has a positive or negative impact on them is entirely up to you. I will close with a reminder; leaders are not only developing their subordinates as employees, you are developing spouses, parents and friends. Your actions towards them in the workplace and how you handle situations that arise will have a direct impact on their spouse and their children once they get home.

My First Situation

The very first story I can recall having to deal with was no small incident; one of my Soldiers had been arrested for Driving Under the Influence (DUI). Staff Sergeant Bermudez was a Soldier within my unit that had a tremendous work ethic. He was my "go to" guy when we needed things to get done quickly. He was instrumental at the early part of my command because of the mess that the previous command team had left. As the current Operations NCO, this Staff Sergeant spent many days and long hours developing systems to help us better track unit statistics, created and updated a non-existent filing system and acquire the training records that were not being kept by the previous command.

Although Bermudez was an outstanding and diligent worker, his life at the time was not easy. He and his wife were going through some difficulty. Their child was living with relatives back in the states and was not able to visit regularly. This Staff Sergeant was not the one to complain though. His pride prevented him from airing his issues nor seek out any sort of marriage counseling. He spoke to SFC Wogomon a few times and told *him* that they were having issues but that was about it. SFC Wogomon would frequently ask him about his home life and offer his assistance where he could. After implementing some of the advice that he got from the Detachment Sergeant and his peers, the Staff Sergeant and his wife starting trying to repair their relationship; and it was working.

I received a phone call on a Saturday morning from SFC Wogomon telling me that Bermudez had been arrested Friday night for Driving under the Influence. Bermudez and his wife were out Friday night in Waikiki on a date. He had admitted to having roughly four mixed drinks throughout the night then decided to try and drive home. A Honolulu Police officer pulls him over for speeding but noticed a strong smell of alcohol coming from the car and conducted a field sobriety test. When Bermudez failed the FST, was arrested and taken down to booking and put on a Breathalyzer to record his blood alcohol level, which was .118 at the time of his arrest. Bermudez's wife called SFC Wogomon as her husband was placed in the police car and she was later picked up by a friend. Bermudez posted bail the next day and given his court date.

SFC Wogomon, Bermudez and I all met back at the office that Saturday afternoon so I could send up the Serious Incident Report (SIR) to the Battalion Commander and the SFC Wogomon read Bermudez his counseling statement. That next Monday, I spoke with the Brigade Judge Advocates (the lawyers) for guidance on the how to proceed with administering legal action against the Soldier. They explained to me that they would typically wait until after the verdict from the civilian court is rendered so that's what we did, we waited.

There were many immediate consequences following Bermudez's arrest. We administratively flagged him which prevented him from receiving any sort of favorable action, reenlist or move to another duty station. He lost his driving privileges on military installations for a year. The State of Hawaii mandated he had to have an ignition interlock device installed in his vehicle if he wanted to continue driving on the island before his case was finalized; the ignition interlock system had an initial installation fee and a reoccurring monthly fee that the Soldier had to endure.

Another mandatory consequence associated with any drug or alcohol related offense is enrollment into the Army Substance Abuse Program or ASAP. This program offers educational classes and one on one counseling for Soldiers dealing with substance abuse or have alcohol related incidences. I command direct Bermudez to go to ASAP and schedule his appointments. This incident was my very first experience with ASAP but unfortunately would not be my last. Some of the counselors would come to know me and SFC Wogomon by name. ___A Rehabilitation Team Meeting (RTM) is a group meeting with the violating Soldiers command team, the Soldier and the counselor. This meeting is where the counselor discusses possible treatment options, receives insight and feedback from the Soldiers commander on the way ahead and is where the Soldier and the commander sign the enrollment contract. This contract outlines the agreed upon treatment plan and informs the Soldier that they are not allowed to consume alcohol until after they are dis-enrolled from the program.___ Our first RTM was one I will never forget. Bermudez's demeanor was one of irritation and the counselor's personality was annoying. The counselor spoke with an annoying voice (like Ben Stein), cleared his throat every few seconds and repeated himself over and over again. SFC Wogomon and I looked at each other in amazement but kept our comments to ourselves and left.

Bermudez continued to work within the operations section while he waited for his court date. The Soldier hired a private lawyer at his own expense and started gathering his defense. On the day of his trial, the HPD officer who made the arrest did not show, the case was dismissed without prejudice and the Soldier was released. SFC Wogomon lifted his administrative flag and thought the matter was concluded. Unfortunately, this was not the case for long. We learned that the State of Hawaii reserves the right to recall a case if it was dismissed without prejudice; and that's what they did so Bermudez received a second summons and a new court date.

Bermudez was attending his ASAP classes and counseling sessions on a regular basis for a year. ***Another RTM is required at the completion of the ASAP program and requires the commander who initially enrolled them, to dis-enroll them.*** SFC Wogomon and I met with the same strange counselor and Bermudez for the results. The counselor gave the recommendation to dis-enroll the Soldier from the program and label it a successful rehabilitation. I asked Bermudez a few of my own questions, to include asking whether or not he had any alcohol while he was still on the program. He went on to explain that he did have some drinks at a couple of social occasions, to include a holiday party over the Christmas holiday. Bermudez talked about how he "was a man" and could control himself. His pride, my no tolerance position against DUIs and the nonchalant manner in which he was telling this story truly bothered me. I lit into that Soldier with a ferocity that surprised me. It wasn't so much that he drank while he was on the program, but the risk and stance he took when he made that decision to violate the rules. I did not allow him to dis-enroll from the program, but instead forced him to remain for another six weeks. I also dictated that he attend Alcohol Anonymous (AA) twice a week while he was still on the program.

Bermudez's second court date finally came around. By this time, Bermudez had received his General Officer Memorandum of Reprimand (GOMOR), his driving privileges had been restored and he no longer had to have the ignition interlock system installed in his vehicle. I recommended his GOMAR be placed in his performance file and my superiors agreed with my recommendation. ***Future leaders, keep in mind that it is often your decision/recommendation that is echoed through you superiors to the final Decision Making Authority. You are in a leadership position because they trust your abilities and impartiality to make the hard choices and will typically back your decision.*** This was a complicated decision because of the second and third order effects it could have. Filing the GOMOR in the performance section carried with it the strong chance of Bermudez not being promoted and ultimately separated from the Army. Although, I didn't think he should be separated from the service, I stood by my original position of "no tolerance" and recommended filing the GOMOR in the section of his file where the next promotion board would see it.

At his hearing, the arresting HPD officer failed to appear for a second time. The case was dismissed a second time but this time it was dismissed *with* prejudice and a final disposition of *Not Guilty*. This verdict still proved not to be the end of this year long endeavor. The Battalion welcomed a new Commander and a new Command Sergeant Major. The new Battalion Commander's (BC) prerogative was that all drug and alcohol related offenses would be adjudicated at her level. After hearing about the *Not Guilty* verdict, the BC's plan of action was to give Bermudez a Field Grade Article 15 and separate him from service. Bermudez was preparing to deploy to Afghanistan at the end of the year, so this plan came as a shock and potentially through a big monkey wrench into our plan. The way ahead became even more convoluted when the Brigade Judge Advocate advised the BC that she could not give the Soldier an Article 15 because of the

Not Guilty verdict but could separate him from the service on the basis that the Soldier received a GOMOR. The BC was adamant about her plan of action and wanted Bermudez out of the army. The hang up was the *Not Guilty* verdict. Bermudez submitted paperwork requesting that his GOMOR be withdrawn since he was found *Not Guilty*. The BC agreed to wait on taking action until the General decided whether or not to remove the GOMOR. If the GOMOR is removed, the Soldier will stay in the military. If the GOMOR is not removed Bermudez will be separated from the service with a General or Other than Honorable characterization of service. Either of these characterizations of service will have a negative impact on Bermudez's ability to obtain civilian employment. This case has been ongoing for over a year and still has not been finalized when I started writing this book.

A hard lessoned learned was not to wait for the state judicial system to administer punishment. I would give the Soldier an Article 15 immediately and let them deal with anything else the State throws at them. Although Bermudez is a good Soldier and think his retention in the Army is warranted, he is on the brink of actually getting away with a DUI and there's not much else I can do about it. I don't know if his GOMOR ever got lifted. This ordeal went on so long that the new Commander inherited this issue.

DEVELOPMENTAL COUNSELING FORM
For use of this form, see FM 6-22; the proponent agency is TRADOC

DATA REQUIRED BY THE PRIVACY ACT OF 1974

AUTHORITY:	5 USC 301, Departmental Regulations; 10 USC 3013, Secretary of the Army.
PRINCIPAL PURPOSE:	To assist leaders in conducting and recording counseling data pertaining to subordinates.
ROUTINE USES:	The DoD Blanket Routine Uses set forth at the beginning of the Army's compilation of systems or records notices also apply to this system.
DISCLOSURE:	Disclosure is voluntary.

PART I - ADMINISTRATIVE DATA

Name (Last, First, MI)	Rank/Grade	Date of Counseling
██████ Bermudez	SSG/E6	████ 2011

Organization	Name and Title of Counselor
13th Military Police Detachment, 728th Military Police Battalion	SFC Wogomon, Stephen H., Detachment Sergeant

PART II - BACKGROUND INFORMATION

Purpose of Counseling: (Leader states the reason for the counseling, e.g. Performance/Professional or Event-Oriented counseling, and includes the leader's facts and observations prior to the counseling.)

Event Oriented Counseling- o Driving Under the Influence Charge by Hawaii Police Department, Blood Alcohol Content(BAC) was .118

PART III - SUMMARY OF COUNSELING
Complete this section during or immediately subsequent to counseling.

Key Points of Discussion:

SSG ██████ you were arrested and charged with Driving Under the Influence on Saturday ██████ 2011 at 0525HRS. Your BAC level was .118, .038 over the legal limit. There is a zero tolerance for drinking and driving. Making the decision to drive a motor vehicle after consuming alcoholic beverages is life altering. Although you may think that this is the worse possible thing that could've happened, it could've been far worse. You put your life, your wife's life and every life of the other drivers on the road at risk. Life is far too short to be ended by poor decision making.

I am fully aware that your are going through rough times at home and the pressures of work are mounting. However this is an attributing factor to going out and "blowing off steam", it cannot be used as an excuse. You know that you can call me anytime day or night. The Commander has also put out several times that Soldiers should make every effort to contact their supervisors when they find themselves in a tight spot and need a ride. Most importantly you have put that same information out to your subordinates.

SSG ██████ you are an extremely important part of this organization and although had a serious lapse in judgment in your decision making, the Commander and I will assist you in every way we can to help you get through this rough time!

I am counseling you for the conduct noted above. If this conduct continues, action may be initiated to separate you from the Army under AR 635-200, Chapters 5, 9, 13, or 14. If you are involuntarily separated, you could receive an Honorable discharge, a General, under honorable conditions, discharge, or an Under Other Than Honorable conditions discharge. An Honorable discharge may be awarded under any provision. A General discharge may be awarded for separation under Chapters 5, 9, 13, and 14. An Under Other Than Honorable conditions discharge may be awarded for separation under Chapter 14. If you receive an Honorable discharge, you will be qualified for most benefits resulting from military service. An involuntary Honorable discharge, however, will disqualify you from reenlistment for some period of time and may disqualify you from receiving transitional benefits (e.g., commissary, housing, health benefits) and the Montgomery GI Bill/Post 911 GI Bill. If you receive a General discharge, you will be disqualified from reenlisting in the service for some period of time and you will be ineligible for some benefits including the Montgomery GI bill. If you receive an Under Other Than Honorable conditions discharge, you will be ineligible for reenlistment and for most benefits including payment for accrued leave, transportation of dependents and household goods to home, transitional benefits and the Montgomery GI Bill/Post 911 GI Bill. You may also face difficulty in obtaining civilian employment, as employers have a low regard for the General and Under Other Than Honorable conditions discharges. Although there are agencies to which you may apply to have the character of your discharge changed, it is unlikely that any such applications will be successful.

OTHER INSTRUCTIONS
This form will be destroyed upon: reassignment   (other than rehabilitative transfers) , separation at ETS, or upon retirement. For separation requirements and notification of loss of benefits/consequences see local directives and AR 635-200.

DA FORM 4856, AUG 2010   PREVIOUS EDITIONS ARE OBSOLETE   APD PE v1.00ES

A Senior NCOs Plight

One of my favorite books, and one that I recommend you read, is *The 48 Laws of Power* by Robert Greene. One of the rules the book discusses is "Keep Your Hands Clean." This next story describes how a senior NCO, SFC Clark, violated that rule and the consequences that came afterward.

I had the unique experience and privilege to command a unit that had Military Working Dogs which was headed up by SFC Clark as its Kennel Master. The kennel section had issues in the past and I knew it would have to be one of my primary focuses at the beginning of my command. I didn't know how bad off the section was when I first took over but I soon found out. There was one Sergeant (SGT Dawson) within the kennel, a dog handler that was removed from his dog because of incidents involving disrespect, failure to obey an order and leaving his post earlier than he was supposed to. SGT Dawson was moved out of the section and was nearing his time to leave the island so an evaluation report was needed from the Kennel Master before he could go. The evaluation report that was initially generated sparked a fiery controversy that brought several skeletons out of the closet. The evaluation report that the Kennel Master generated was a "Relief for Cause" NCOER (Non Commissioned Officer Evaluation Report). A RFC NCOER is a very bad evaluation and is detrimental for a Soldier to become promotable in the future. One of the issues in this case is that many of the comments on the NCOER did not have any previous negative counseling statements to support what was written on the evaluation. This NCOER was filled with negative comments and depicted Dawson in a very negative light. SFC Wogomon told Clark that he would have to modify the NCOER and that it couldn't be a "Relief for Cause," that he still had to put on the evaluation the positive things the Soldier did or accomplished. Clark took the criticism and started making the corrections to the NCOER but is not enough for Dawson.

I was sitting in my office when Dawson knocked on my door and tells me that he wants to use the Battalion Sergeant Majors open door policy. I appreciated the heads up and not being blindsided by my superiors on any issues that Dawson might bring up. Dawson wanted to talk about Clark and let some stuff "out of the bag" and warned him the way he delivered his information to the Sergeant Major would be critical; not everything on his negative NCOER was false and if he wasn't careful, his statements would be viewed as an attempt to falsely incriminate a senior Noncommissioned Officer that was giving him a bad rating. I proceeded to tell him it was his right to go and see the Sergeant Major if he liked but I asked him if he would possibly allow me the opportunity to address his issues. Dawson proceeded to elaborate on a lot of negative things about the kennel and his supervisors, as I knew he would, but then makes a statement that caught me off guard. Within the plethora of accusations he was making, he states that Clark used his rank and position for personal gain. Confusion fell across my face and then ask him to elaborate on what he meant by his comment. He told me:

A fellow dog handler who was also a Sergeant, E-5, pulls his truck into the fenced compound of the kennel. The Soldier was quite upset due to the fact that someone had keyed the hood and driver side of his vehicle. Clark came out to look at the vehicle and they called someone from the Provost Marshals Office (military police station) to come out and document the damage so the Soldier could file an insurance claim. The Military Police Soldier shows up with his camera to document the damage. As the MP is taking photos, the Soldier asks Clark *"How do I get the whole truck painted?"* Clark quickly replies back with *"You've got to key the whole truck."* This response confused the young Sergeant as he stood there contemplating the response. He finally looks up at Clark, with his keys in hand, and says *"I can't key my own truck, Sergeant."* They stand and look at each other for a minute; finally Clark takes the keys from the Sergeant and proceeds to key the passenger and tail end of the Sergeants truck. After he is finished, Clark looked over to the MP, who is a Specialist (E-4) and says *"All four sides were keyed, right?"* The Specialist nods in understanding and generates a police report indicating that all sides were damaged. The Soldier submitted his claim and the falsified police report to his insurance company and gets his entire truck painted.

After this elaborate story, the Sergeant in question just happened to be up at the Detachment. I asked him to step into the office then asked him if Clark keyed his vehicle. The Soldier didn't say a word but didn't have to, his face flushed and his mouth almost fell open, so I stated *"So he did then"* and let the Soldier be on his way. Soon after the nonverbal acknowledgment from the Soldier, I informed the Battalion Commander of the situation then went over to Brigade JAG (the lawyers) for legal advice on how to proceed. I issued a "no contact" order to Clark, the Sergeant who owned the vehicle in question and Dawson. ___A "no-contact" order prohibits the recipients of the order from engaging in any type of conversation; no phone, text, face to face,___

social media, no contact what so ever. The recipients can be charged
with Article 92 (Failure to obey an order or regulation) which is
punishable under the Uniform Code of Military Justice (UCMJ).

The Kennel Master position is held by a Soldier in the rank of Sergeant First Class (E-7). A SFC can receive an Article 15 at any level, from Company/Detachment to a Field Grade Article 15 but neither of those convening authorities can take their rank. Keeping this in mind, the Brigade Commander felt it appropriate to keep the investigation and disposition of this case at her level. An Investigating Officer from the Brigade was appointed and Clark was suspended from his duties pending the outcome of the investigation. Upon his suspension, Clark posted a negative comment on Facebook, stating *"I no longer have faith in my Command Team"* and then all of the subsequent questions and comments from his friends started coming in.

During the investigation, the MP Specialist who submitted the false report admitted to and confirmed the entire recollection of events as it was initially told by the disgruntled Sergeant Dawson. Clark fought and tap danced all over the place, admitting to keying the vehicle but only keying the portions that were already keyed; making the comment that they were just having fun and that the Soldier gave him permission to key his truck. When Clark told me this, I fired back at him the question *"How is that fun? Is that the professional thing to do? If I gave you permission to slash my tires, how's that going to look to the witnesses around my vehicle?"* The Sergeant who owned the vehicle invoked his rights and refused to make any comments.

At the end of the investigation, it was the final determination that Clark did key the vehicle and that the MP Specialist submitted a false report but there was no hard physical evidence to warrant an Article 15.

Clark, the Sergeant who owned the vehicle and the MP Specialist all got a Letter of Reprimand (LoR) form the Brigade Commander. Once these letters were issued verbally to the offenders, I had to provide a recommendation on how the LoR would be filed. I recommended that the Clark's LoR be filed in his performance file. I recommended that the junior Sergeants LoR be filed in the restricted portion of his file. I felt the Sergeant was given a poor example to follow, guided down the wrong path and being brought onto the Brigade Commanders "carpet" would be enough to set him on to the right path. The MP Specialist, whom I believe is the worst offender in this entire case, was on his last days in the Army. I recommended that his LoR be filed in the performance section of his file but this still would not affect the Soldier. I was the one to read him his letter from the Brigade Commander and proceeded to tell him what I thought of him and his actions. His lack of integrity brought dishonor to the entire Military Police Corps and the Army is a better organization without him.

After the case finalized, Clark was moved out of the section and over to another sister unit within the Battalion. As his rater, I had to provide him with his NCOER before he transitioned to the other unit. On the front of an NCOER is a list of all the Army Values with a check box "Yes" or "No" beside each value. I checked "No" beside the Value "Loyalty", knowing that would more than likely affect his ability to be promoted to Master Sergeant (E-8). The Facebook comment that he posted earlier was the reason I checked this block. Not only was the comment detrimental to good order and discipline, but he had his subordinate Soldiers, which means they were my subordinate Soldiers as friends on his Facebook page. This was not something I was going to tolerate. *Leaders, DO NOT be friends with your subordinates on any social media sites!* Clark was not happy at all with the outcome of neither the investigation nor his NCOER. Although he was already selected for promotion, he feared that a Stand By Advisory Board (STAB) would be convened and remove his promotable status. If he was removed from the list, he would be nearing the length of time he could remain a SFC, ultimately ending his time in the Army. He came to me asking to change the report but I refused. With the negative NCOER pending, the Letter of Reprimand in his file and the possibility of losing his promotable status, the Kennel Master wrote his congressman and outlined his situation. The Congressman's office sent a letter of inquiry into the matter which required a very prompt response. Clark's words to his Congressman described all of his leadership as unfair and that he was being treated with much disdain. I provided all of the documentation I had on Clark to the Battalion Commander who drafted the response back to the Congressman's office. The Congressman was content with our answers and the due process that Clark was afforded.

Clark was finally moved to the other unit, the case closed and Clark waited for what was to come of his promotion. He was indeed promoted to the rank of Master Sergeant and works as an Operations NCO for that unit and is doing well. Although he was very upset at the events that unfolded, the Soldier's resiliency was of note; he did not let the looming circumstances surrounding him affect his work performance. Good for him.

*The following is an excerpt from the letter that Clark wrote to his Congressman. In the letter, he goes on to admit that he did key the Soldiers truck. *

Apparently, I am being investigated for alleged fraud, stemming from a ▇▇▇▇ 2011 incident, at which time I scratched my soldier, ▇▇▇▇'s truck.

Background:

On ▇▇▇▇, SGT ▇▇▇▇ 2008 ▇▇▇▇ Chevy ▇▇▇▇ vandalized (keyed) outside of his Barracks building #774. Upon discovery of the vandalism that same night, ▇▇▇▇ called the Schofield Barracks Military Police and filed a Military Police Report (▇▇▇▇ ▇▇▇▇). The report was filed at 1800 hours and completed at 1830 hours; again, on the same night that the incident took place. Due to lack of sufficient light, attempts to photograph the damage were unsuccessful that night; therefore a follow up report was scheduled for the next day.

On ▇▇▇▇, 2011, between the hours of approximately 0930 and 1130 hours, SGT ▇▇▇▇ pulled into the Military Working Dog Kennel facility. SGT ▇▇▇▇ and I began to casually talk about his truck and he explained that he already called his insurance company that morning and filed his claim for the damage. This was the first time I saw the vehicle, since learning about the damage that morning, at Physical Training formation. Looking at the vehicle, I could see scratches in the paint down the driver's side, across the hood and down the passenger side of the. We talked about his vehicle some more and SGT ▇▇▇▇ stated that someone would be coming over from the M.P. Station to do the follow up pictures later that day. We talked a little more, and I walked back inside the building, to continue working. Between approximately 1230 and 1300 hours, I went back outside and began talking with SGT ▇▇▇▇ again. He stated that SPC ▇▇▇▇ from the MP desk had come over to take pictures in the daylight of the vehicle.) He stated At some point in our conversation, SGT ▇▇▇▇ stated that the entire truck would have to be repainted again, since the damage was so extensive. In jest I joked that he should just "junk it." He and I both laughed, and he said something to the effect of, "Just go ahead and mess it up, I don't care?" Laughing again, I scratched his vehicle. We both laughed about it, and he said he didn't, care, since the truck would have to be completely repainted anyway. Afterwards, we laughed, shared the joke with our co-workers and went back to work.

On ▇▇▇▇ 2011, four months after the mentioned incident, I was informed by a few junior soldiers, that my Commander and 1SG were inquiring into the incident between SGT

Assault on Man's Best Friend

This next case is definitely out of the ordinary and cannot say I thought I would ever have to deal with a situation like this. One Wednesday morning, SFC Wogomon, pulled me to the side and proceeds to tell me that we are losing a handler (Military Working Dog Handler). I look at him with confusion, and ask him *"why, what happened?"* *"SSG Braxton punched his dog in the face."* He replied.

That morning, the Military Working Dog section was conducting PT (Physical Training) with their dogs. They were doing PT on a very common run route; there were a lot of Soldiers out that day. I even ran past them with one of my fellow commanders. The handlers were subjected to many different muscle failure and cardiovascular exercises. The stipulation was added that their Military Working Dog had to lie down or sit and not move until the handler completed their exercise. If the dog broke from their position, the handler had to knock out another 10 pushups on top of the exercise they just had to complete. With that said, there was one handler that was having difficulty keeping his dog in the desired position and the handler had to pay the consequence of doing the additional pushups. During another set of exercises, the dog broke from its position again, came to the handler in a playful manner and somehow scratched the handler in the face. The handler then lost his composure, rears back and strikes the dog in the face. Now it's bad enough that the handler hit the dog, but it makes it much worse to misbehave in public as a Military Police Soldier.

Later, I went to inform the Battalion Commander what had happened. I told her that I didn't have all of the specifics as of yet because SFC Wogomon was still doing some fact finding. I didn't want her to be blindsided, however, if she got a phone call about the incident since it occurred in a very crowded area. She was not at all pleased and was just as surprised that it happened as I was. *I have found the most Soldiers, both officer and enlisted, are dog lovers.*

After all the details had been obtained, the story had changed from SSG Braxton *punched* the dog to SSG Braxton slapped the dog with an open hand strike. I called the Brigade legal team for some advice on how to proceed. SSG Braxton was already going to be removed from his dog and from the kennel. He was also going to receive a negative evaluation report due to the incident. At the time, I initially felt some sort of punitive action should be taken for the event. There is a charge within the Uniform Code of Military Justice (UCMJ) that outlines such a charge. ***Article 134 is a general article that covers many acts of misconduct. One such charge is "Abuse to a Public Animal." The term "public" refers to an animal that is used by the government for official purposes (i.e. a Military Working Dog).*** I felt that a Summarized Article 15 would be appropriate. I did not intend to take the Soldiers money or give him extra duty; my intent was to issue him a Letter of Reprimand (LoR) that would be filed locally.

When I briefed the boss and the Command Sergeant Major (CSM) my intent, the CSM gave guidance that I could still give a LoR without the Article 15. Doing an Article 15 would delay the process of moving the Soldier out of the unit and into a new one. I agreed and decided not to process an Article 15 for the event, just write and issue SSG Braxton the LoR.

This issue was resolved before the close of business (COB) that same day. SSG Braxton was not allowed to return to the kennels except to turn his stuff in. I gave the Soldier his LoR and he was in a new unit the next morning.

Homosexual Love Triangle

I was in a huddle in my office one day with a couple of my Soldiers discussing the upcoming Unit Strength Report (USR) meeting when one of the First Sergeants (1SG) from a sister unit, 1SG Eddy, came into my office with an expression of frustration and anger. I asked *"You need a minute?"* He shook his *"yes sir,"* the two Soldiers excused themselves and the 1SG shut the door. He sat down and asked me to give a "no contact" order to one of my Soldiers. He explained that my Soldier, PVT Wilson, was sending text messages to a Platoon Sergeant without any regard to customs or courtesies. This, however, was not the root cause of his frustration.

Both PVT Wilson and his Soldier, PVT Iwan, were romantically involved. This relationship was not only romantic, but sexual. What really surprised me was when the 1SG told me that the other Soldier in question was also a guy. This homosexual relationship had been going on for an unknown amount of time but soon to come to an end when PVT Iwan got married. This did not go over to well with PVT Wilson at all. He tried to stop the wedding by telling his lover's fiancé that the man she was to marry was gay. This didn't, however, deter the woman from marrying PVT Iwan anyway.

It is unknown yet suspected that the two Soldiers are still having some sort of discrete affair but it wasn't confirmed. What is known is that the Soldiers were still in communication and the now married PVT Iwan was confiding all his marital issues in his ex-lover. This is when PVT Wilson sent a text message to his ex-lover's Platoon

Sergeant, stating that he needed to bring PVT Iwan by so he could get some things off of his chest. The married couple was also receiving other outside pressures from other Soldiers as well. Other Soldiers from the same unit as PVT Iwan were offering his wife a "contract marriage" if things between her and her bi-sexual husband didn't work out. The command team of those Soldiers issued a "no contact" order, preventing them from having any contact with the wife. This infuriated the wife. The wife called the command team, telling them that had no right; that they were taking away her friends. *Although she was not happy, this was still a good decision made by this command team. These Soldiers contact with the couple was detrimental to the good order and discipline within that unit.*

The tactless and disrespectful text and the numerous phone calls from the wife drove 1SG Eddy to try and intervene into the situation in some way. He had had enough and was trying to do whatever he could to mitigate further issues. In regards to his request to issue a "no contact" order, I felt that this wouldn't be the appropriate course of action to deal with the situation. The Soldiers in question did not do anything wrong at this point nor did PVT Iwan or his spouse request that PVT Wilson stop contacting them. The ex-lovers continued contact is not illegal and was not, at that time, detrimental to good order and discipline. We counseled PVT Wilson on appropriate relationships within the service and informed them that male on male sexual contact is still considered adultery since PVT Iwan was married and could be charged as such if they were caught.

__Leaders, "no contact" orders are resourceful and effective tools you can use to try and mitigate the escalation of a situation. The order also provides legal grounds to charge a Soldier who__ *violates the order with Article 92 of the UCMJ—Failure to Obey an Order or Regulation. Keep in mind, however, that a "no contact" order can't be used all the time. The Army is not in the business of determining who Soldiers can and cannot be friends with. Leaders must also keep in mind that a "no contact" order is only a temporary measure. The leadership must initiate some kind of action that generates a more long term solution. Don't confuse this with a Military Protective Order (MPO). An MPO is the equivalent to a civilian restraining order and have harsher consequences if violated. "No contact" orders can be given if:*

- *A Soldier is under investigation—A "no contact" order can be issued preventing the Soldier from interacting with other subjects associated with that investigation until the investigation is concluded.*
- *A Soldier has engaged in an inappropriate relationship of some kind; they can be ordered to stay away from the other party in the relationship.*
- *Contact between two Soldiers becomes a detriment to good order and discipline within the unit.*

Consult your legal representative or Inspector General (IG) for more guidance if you are unsure on how to implement this order, an MPO or whether or not issuing such an order is legal.

The next day, I was told that the other unit had issued a "no contact" order PVT Iwan anyway, preventing him from having any contact with PVT Wilson, devastating PVT Wilson and pushing him closer to a breaking point. PVT Wilson felt like his best friend and this person that he loved had been taken away from him permanently. We also came do discover that PVT Wilson had posted some comments on Facebook that caused alarm to some of his friends. One of his friends calls him to ask if everything was alright and asks him *"you're not thinking about hurting yourself are you?"* PVT Wilson replied *"no, that was last week."* After they get off the phone, the concerned friend calls another Sergeant within my unit and told him about the conversation that he just had with PVT Wilson. The Sergeant heads up stairs and informed SFC Wogomon about the comments that PVT Wilson made. SFC Wogomon called the PVT Wilson and his supervisor to his office and has a very long conversation with Wilson. During this hour long conversation, Wilson had admitted that the thought of suicide had crossed his mind and that he had a plan on how to carry it out; that he was going to use the gun that is kept at the Police Desk and blow his brains out.

__Suicidal ideations are another leadership challenge that must be handled smartly, delicately and quickly. First, you don't want to leave the Soldier alone; suicide watch for at least 24 hours is essential. The next step is a referral to a mental health provider for evaluation. The provider will give recommendations to the commander on how to proceed with handling the Soldier. It is recommended that the Soldier remain under constant supervision until the results from the doctor are received.__ In this case, the provider recommended that PVT Wilson's access to weapons and ammunition be restricted and regular appointments be established for PVT Wilson to continue seeing the therapist. We complied with the doctors recommendations, removed him from his Law Enforcement duties and ensured that he made his appointments.

In most cases, suicidal ideations warrant a Serious Incident Report (SIR) to your higher echelon commander(s); ensure that you are keeping them in the loop. It will not bode well for you if a Soldier does end up attempting or committing suicide and your commander finds out that you knew that it was a possibility. You might as well pack your office up; you will be relieved.

Wilson was watched a little more closely and given different duties and responsibilities within the police station, just nothing around weapons or ammunition. Wilson ended up doing really well in his new job. He fought the transition at first but ended up being successful. He doesn't have any more contact with Iwan and that's probably for the best. Wilson made all of his therapy appointments and was soon to be cleared to return to all of his previous Law Enforcement duties.

The Bigamist

The offender in this next story is SPC Long. SPC Long performed many functions when I first took command of my unit. Long was a traffic accident investigator, the unit armorer and a Special Reaction Team (military version of SWAT) member. It wasn't until a few weeks into my command that I started to notice this Soldier's performance was not up to par and that his critical thinking capabilities were extremely low. The first time a red flag went off in my head about this kid was when the arms room paperwork was not in order. The arms room, where we keep our weapons and ammunition, is NOT a place where errors in judgment and documentation can be made. Long struck me as a humble yet simple person; young and inexperienced in the Army and in life.

SPC Long was married to a young girl who had severe trust issues and was constantly hounding SPC Long about where he had been, who he was with and what he was doing. SPC Long could not even mention that one of his co-workers happened to be female without her flipping out. His wife would even come to the Provost Marshals Office (police station) to check up on him. She had even been known at times to follow him around while he was out on patrol. This girl was extremely jealous and emotionally troubled.

The wife's father added an interesting dynamic into the situation due to the fact he too was in the Army. He just so happened to be a Lieutenant Colonel (LTC) chaplain that was stationed on the island but moved to another duty station stateside. His daughter was enrolled in college courses at the University of Hawaii and had stayed back to go to school.

The marriage took both families by surprise. These two love birds decided it would be the better idea to elope but failed to inform either family about their plans. Although disappointed, both families supported their matrimony and did what they could to assist the newlyweds. It wasn't soon after this, however, that the two started having problems. The wife's jealousy erupted and their fights were emotionally abusive on both their parts. The wife would report their issues to her father, which in turn would try and offer advice on how to fix their issues. After dealing with their issues from afar, the father finally called me. He had elaborated a little more on their home life issues to try and give me a better understanding about what they were going through. I told the chaplain that I would support the couple in any way that I could. The second phone call I had received from her dad stopped me in my tracks. The chaplain had set up a counseling session with a peer chaplain who worked in the 25th Infantry Division and wanted to be sure that it was ok with me and asked that I provided Long the time needed to attend this couples counseling session. He was telling me about some of the things that his daughter had been reporting to him and what SPC Long was doing and how he was being emotionally abusive. I fired back and tried to let him know that his daughter's actions at times were just as abusive. The chaplain retaliated with a statement that proclaimed him the victor of that conversation. He told me that the biggest catalyst for their arguments is because SPC Long was still married to another woman!

I called Long to my office, sat him down and ask him directly, *"Are you still married to your first wife?"* He replies without hesitation but with reservation *"Yes sir."* *"Explain"* I say. He proceeded to tell me that his first wife petitioned for divorce in her home state and sent the papers to Hawaii for Long to sign. He mailed the signed papers back to his first wife but didn't check up on the status. He just signed, mailed and assumed that the situation would take care of itself. He got married to the second wife, thinking he was divorced, free and clear of his first wife. The reality of the situation was the first wife never filed the signed documents to the court. I asked him, why doesn't she just file the papers now? *"They were destroyed"* he said. *"My mom is coming out to the island and she is bringing new ones for me to sign."*

I found myself at another decision point that required reflection and consultation with SFC Wogomon, the Brigade legal team and the acting Battalion Commander. Long's mother even came to my office on her sons behalf to explain her version of the situation. She broke down and cried as she was describing the stressful and strained relationship that was their marriage. ***Leaders, keep in mind that you should not be the one asking the questions to your subordinates. As the adjudicator, you must remain impartial and out of the investigatory process. This is an incident where I would not repeat my course of action. The proper answer would have been to initiate a commander's inquiry, have an investigating officer appointed and allow them to conduct the investigation.*** After much discussion and guidance from the lawyers, my boss and SFC Wogomon, I concluded that the marriage to the second wife was not malicious in nature nor was an attempt to defraud the second wife or the government so I cut Long a little slack. I counseled him on the offense of Bigamy and had him administratively flagged so he could not receive any sort of favorable action until he was divorced from the first wife. I did not, however, give the Soldier an Article 15, I allowed him the opportunity to fix his situation.

As much as I wish I could stop writing after such an account of stupidity and drama, there is unfortunately more to tell and more I had to deal with. A couple weeks later, the wife petitions the State of Hawaii for a restraining order against Long. In the petition, she describes many altercations between the two of them and makes a serious allegation that lands SPC Long in the middle of a CID investigation for sexual assault. ***The Criminal Investigations Division (CID) investigates felony level crimes to include Sexual Assault.*** The wife claimed that Long had, in previous fights, became violent towards her and that one night after a party, he had ejaculated in her mouth after she had passed out from consuming too much alcohol.

Family Advocacy got involved and helped the wife obtain a temporary restraining order (TRO) against SPC Long. The subsequent pages within the TRO described incidences, in her words, where SPC Long had either pushed her, had threatened to do her physical harm or both. One account described how he threw a GNC shaker at her foot so hard that she had to receive medical treatment from the health clinic. Long claimed that he only meant to throw the cup to the ground after she had spilt water on him and the cup accidently hit her foot. ***Leaders, although the military falls under a federal legal system, you are still required to ensure your Soldiers comply with any mandate or order that comes from a State court. Those Soldiers who think that the military can't intervene in a State matter are sorely mistaken. One way to approach this is to tell your Soldier to comply with the law. This is a legal, moral and ethical order. If they fail to comply, you could charge them***

with UCMJ Article 92—Failure to Obey a Direct Order or Regulation.

After CID completed their investigation, it was determined that there was not enough evidence to prosecute Long for any indecent acts or sexual assault. The investigators did, however, conclude that Long was guilty of Assault and Battery when he threw the GNC shaker and it hit his wife's foot. In light of their findings, I issued an Article 15 to the Soldier for Assault and Battery to his wife. We also required him to go to Anger Management courses offered on post. **_Anger Management is another resource a leader can make mandatory if a Soldier displays constant hostility or makes a poor decision out of anger. Most posts offer this service. Other sources of counseling are the Military Family Life Consultant (MFLC) or your unit Chaplain._**

SPC Long was soon after divorced from his first wife. His mom ensured that the papers were filed this time by filing them herself. The marriage between Long and the second wife was not repairable either so steps were taken to have it annulled. I still received regular phone calls from the father inquiring about the status of the court case. I told him that I would not give any orders to Long regarding the legal proceedings he had with the second wife; this was now a civil matter. He was legally married to only one woman and any legal proceedings between him and his second wife was not my business. I did tell him that I would talk to the Soldier about the importance of not dragging his feet on this and getting it closed out. The father would even call Long's lawyer to get updates and gave them my number. Long's lawyers called me when they couldn't get a hold of him or to tell me that he was procrastinating. Finally, after being delayed for weeks, the court case was heard, the marriage was annulled and Long is wifeless—as far as I know.

* The following supporting document is an excerpt from the second wife's restraining order petition she filed with the State of Hawaii. This is only one page of a very long and explicit document.*

5. The Respondent has abused the Petitioner and/or the above listed family/household member(s) as follows:

A. FIRST INCIDENT OF ABUSE

Respondent abused ☒ me and/or _____

on (date) ~~██████~~ January ██ by ☒ doing or ☐ threatening to do this:

☐ choke ☐ force to have sex ☐ grab ☐ hit ☐ kick ☐ slap ☐ punch ☐ push ☒ shove ☐ other _____

briefly describe this incident: We were in a heated argument and he Shoved me so hard I lost my balance and fell on Floor. He didn't help me up. He walked away.

This was: ☒ physical harm; ☐ threat of imminent physical harm, bodily injury, assault;
☐ extreme psychological abuse; ☐ malicious property damage.

These children were in the home, were close by, or were present when the above incident occurred:

_____

B. MOST RECENT INCIDENT OF ABUSE (check here if same as above ☐)

Respondent abused ☒ me and/or _____

on (date) August 5 ████ by ☒ doing or ☒ threatening to do this:

☐ choke ☐ force to have sex ☐ grab ☐ hit ☐ kick ☐ slap ☒ punch ☐ push ☒ shove ☐ other

briefly describe this incident: We were in a heated argument Walking home from Commissary and he didn't like that I was walking instead of driving so he started yelling and cussing at me. He said he wanted to punch me in my face and instead Shoved me hard

This was: ☒ physical harm; ☒ threat of imminent physical harm, bodily injury, assault;
☐ extreme psychological abuse; ☐ malicious property damage.

These children were in the home, were close by, or were present when the above incident occurred:

_____

C. OTHER INCIDENT(S) OF ABUSE (attach continuation page(s) if needed)

Respondent abused ☒ me and/or _____

on (date) June ████ by ☒ doing or ☐ threatening to do this:

☐ choke ☐ force to have sex ☐ grab ☐ hit ☐ kick ☐ slap ☐ punch ☐ push ☐ shove ☒ other

briefly describe this incident: We were in a heated argument and I accidentally spilled water on him and he grabbed the gac Shaker that was Filled with water and smashed it on my Foot. I had to go to the Acute Clinic on base the next day

This was: ☒ physical harm; ☐ threat of imminent physical harm, bodily injury...

A Drug Addict

This story is about a very young private named PVT Davidson. Davidson was given to me in an effort to provide one of our under strength sections with a little help. Davidson's previous leadership bamboozled me by giving up this particular Soldier to "help". He ended up being one of the biggest detriments to the unit and a person and family that I lost every ounce of respect for.

Davidson comes off as a simple minded "country bumpkin" that acts like he fell of the hay ride one too many times. This 23 year old kid was already married and had conceived a child. Davidson's life growing up wasn't a picture perfect; his mom was a drug addict, his father was not around and his grandmother who raised him, had recently passed away. His attitude on the other hand seemed relatively positive. He seemed to be driven to succeed and had good intentions but I would soon discover that it was all a farce.

PVT Davidson had already received an Article 15 from his previous Company Commander before coming over to me. He received the Article 15 because he couldn't seem to get up and to formation on time in the mornings. I will admit at times, and sometimes to my detriment, that I am the optimist and a little gullible. This Soldier's display of ignorant innocence made me feel a little empathetic towards him. I gave him the benefit of the doubt on more than one occasion. Davidson also had documented medical problems in regards to his hearing. Davidson was almost deaf in one ear. Naturally, I associated him not getting up on time to his hearing loss and possibly not being able to hear his alarm. *__The Soldier was counseled in writing each time he was late. Valid excuse or not, written documentation followed by counseling session is imperative if the problem continues or the valid excuses turn out to be lies.__* We cut Davidson a little slack because of his hearing issue and figured the situation would rectify itself when Davidson was outfitted with a hearing aid which he was already scheduled for. In the meantime, we suggested that he get a second alarm clock and/or have his wife help him get up in the morning.

All Department of Defense employees are subject to random drug tests. *__As a commander, I am required to conduct a random urinalysis of my unit each month and typically get the results back with a couple days via email.__* Names are drawn at random from the Army Substance Abuse Program system to ensure impartiality. Davidson's name was one of the Soldiers on the list; he comes in, pees in a cup and leaves. A couple days later, I open the results email and it is all downhill from this point. Davidson had tested positive for a prescription medication, Oxycontin, which was not prescribed to him.

Soon after the positive drug test, the investigatory process began. A medical professional combed through his medical history for any prescriptions of Oxy but didn't find any. *__Administratively, we flagged Davidson, processed a Field Grade Article 15, Command Referred him to the Army Substance Abuse Program (ASAP) and initiated separation paperwork. Separation initiation is a requirement in the Army for a Soldier that has a positive urinalysis. The Criminal Investigations Division (CID) must also be notified. They will conduct a preliminary investigation into the matter then pass their recommendations to the Commander.__*

***You must also get ASAP involved for any drug or alcohol related
offense.***

PVT Davidson had a seemingly reasonable excuse that could
potentially happen to anyone. His side of the story was that he
woke in the middle of the night in pain. He went to the medicine
cabinet, half asleep, and grabbed a pill bottle that he thought was his.
He unknowingly grabbed his wife's prescription bottle containing
the Oxy; he took the pills and went back to bed. I was somewhat
empathetic to his story because I found myself in a similar situation as
a young Lieutenant.

In 2005, I had a piercing headache that was making me sick to
my stomach and I didn't want to move so I asked my wife to bring me
some medicine. She goes into the bathroom to the medicine cabinet
then brings me some water with two pills. I took them without any
hesitation. About 20 minutes later, I was right as reign and was feeling
really good. I said *"I didn't think Excedrine Migraine worked so fast."*
She looked at me and says *"That wasn't Excedrine, it was my Tylenol."*
My face just sank. She was struggling with a back injury she got while
we were skiing in college and the doctor prescribed her Tylenol 3. If
you are unaware, Tylenol 3 contains Codeine which is a controlled
substance. ***Inform your supervisor immediately and explain the
situation. Ignorance is not a valid excuse but certain situations
are understandable. Ignorance then trying to hide it, however, will
land you in very hot water.***

Davidson, SFC Wogomon and I all headed to the Battalion
Commanders office for his Article 15 reading. ***The Battalion
Command or higher are the adjudicators of Field Grade Article
15's.*** PVT Davidson stood outside the office until he is told to report

to the Battalion Commander. He knocks, and upon permission, he enters, walks up to the "X" on the ground in front of the Lieutenant Colonels desk and salutes.

He proceeded to tell the same story to the boss about how he took the pills on accident. Davidson also had his wife come to testify on his behalf. She stood there with their baby on her hip and told the BC that Davidson's account of what happened was accurate. His wife went on to explain the steps they were taking to mitigate the risks of this ever happening again. After her testimony, the BC dismissed both Davidson and his wife while we discussed his fate. When the BC asked my opinion on the matter, I explained to her that I believed he did take the pills on accident. It is a feasible scenario, his wife corroborated his story and he had no history of drugs use in his file. I recommended that she give him an oral reprimand but not take his money nor rank. The Soldier and his family were already experiencing financial problems and, at that time, I feared that taking his money would be detrimental to the family. The boss agreed and went along with my recommendation. Davidson came back in and stood at attention while the Lieutenant Colonel gives him a bona fide Ass Chewing. She also gives him 45 days of extra duty but suspends it. ***This means that if he were to get in trouble again, the suspension would be lifted and he would receive the 45 days of extra duty on top of the punishment he would get from whatever he was being punished for.***

After the Article 15 reading was over, we all went back up to my office. I talked to both Davidson and his wife for a bit but then asked Davidson to step outside. *I believe that serving in the military requires a family effort.* ***The spouses sacrifice just as much, if not more, for this country. They are also impacted and affected if their Soldier gets***

in trouble. In an attempt to stay true to my philosophy, I unofficially "counsel" Davidson's wife like she was one of my own Soldiers. She sat across the other side of my desk as I explained to her how important it was for her to get involved in her husband's career. I told her that she needed ensure that he gets up on time, that he makes it to work on time and that she become the sense of reason to him that keeps out of trouble. I was very candid with her about what would happen and what I would do if he was not able to get his act together; that I will not hesitate to kick him out of the military if his misconduct continued. She said that she understood and that she would step up and help him stay out of trouble.

SFC Wogomon and I also had to have meeting with Davidson's ASAP counselor to discuss drug treatment options. I explained to the counselor that I did not think any further requirements be placed on him since I was under the impression he took the pills by mistake. *This is a decision I wish I could go back and change.* ***My opinion and recommendation to you future leaders is that you make ASAP a requirement no matter what the circumstances surrounding a drug or alcohol incident.***

Unfortunately, the situation continued to deteriorate even more. Davidson was continuously late to appointments, to formation and his work performance had degraded significantly. The counseling statements from his supervisors were starting to add up. Davidson's financial situation was also getting worse. He came to me to ask for an Army Emergency Relief (AER) loan because he lost his bank card and was unable to pay some of his bills. ***The Army Emergency Relief fund is a charity specifically for Soldiers in need. The money for this fund is provided by generous Soldiers that donate into it.***

I approved his loan request and he was able to pay his outstanding bills. His family life was also getting worse. Davidson and his wife constantly argued, she had threatened to leave him on several occasions, and to top it all off, she was pregnant again.

A few days later, Davidson was out in his car crying his eyes out. A Master Sergeant (MSG) from a sister Company was walking by and saw him. He gets out of his car and asks if he can speak to her. He starts talking about all of his financial problems, marital problems, the fact his wife's pregnant again and all his work related stress. The MSG listens to him vent but realizes that there might be a deeper issue and asks *"You haven't thought about hurting yourself have you?"* Davidson replied in his long southern draw *"well, I've thought about it."* After their conversation, the MSG comes straight to my office and tells me what happened. *Suicidal Ideations are extremely serious and must be handled very quickly.* ___*Preventing that person from being alone is imperative until they are evaluated by a mental health professional. A mental health evaluation must also be done as soon as possible. The psychiatrist will provide their recommendations and the Commander must ensure that the guidelines are adhered to.*___ We do all of this, Davidson was placed on suicide watch for 72 hours and I referred him to Behavioral Health for a mental evaluation. The results from the mental evaluation forced me to truly reevaluate how I look at Soldiers and I learned a hard yet valuable life lesson that day.

It turns out that Davidson not only lied about taking his wife's medication on accident, but that he was popping 4 to 5 pills a day. I lost every ounce of respect for him and his wife after I heard that. They plotted, schemed and fabricated such an elaborate lie in order to get out of this situation. I believe the part that bothers me the most is that the lie was a family effort. I can understand Davidson lying to save his own skin, but to bring his wife and baby into it put it over the top. I recanted my original decision about his attendance at ASAP and made it a requirement for him to go through the program.

After he had been in the ASAP program for a couple days, his counselor called me and said she needed to see me. She wanted to talk to me about signing Davidson up for a treatment plan called TRISAR. She began explaining all of the reasons why this program would be a better treatment plan for Davidson. In her explanation, she revealed that Davidson was not only continuing to "relapse" but this Soldier had been popping pills since before he even came into the Army. As I was listening and trying to put everything into perspective, I found myself becoming more and more infuriated. This Soldier complained about money issues, received money from AER, got food vouchers from the chaplain, both PVT Davidson and his wife were smokers (pack of cigarettes in Hawaii = $8+), his wife was seen eating out at Popeye's on post on a regular basis yet there was no food in the house and he was using his money to go buy pills out in Wahiawa (A Hawaiian ghetto). Davidson and his wife were manipulating and taking advantage of every system that they could.

The revelation of what he had really been doing solidified my course of action that I was going to take with this family: finish the chapter process and recommend that he be discharged from the Army for Serious Misconduct.

While we were waiting on the process of separation to happen and for him to get orders, Davidson still continued to be late to work and to his appointments (medical, ASAP, behavioral health). Davidson's supervisors came to me and explained that none of their corrective actions were working; Davidson was still failing to be where he was supposed to be and recommended that I impose punitive action on the Soldier. Armed with the knowledge that this kid was a drug addict and spending his money on pills, I was not willing to show him any leniency. I decided to give him a Company Grade Article 15. After the Article 15 was read and Davidson had an opportunity to seek legal counsel, it was time to pass my judgment and punishment and I did not hold back. I threw everything within my power at this kid. I reduced him in rank (from Private First Class—E3 to Private—E2), took almost $400 from his next paycheck and gave him 15 days of extra duty. I also went back to the Battalion Commander and asked her to revoke her suspension of his 45 days of extra duty; totaling 60 days this Soldier would be on extra duty. ***Extra duty is a punishment that can be administered if someone is found guilty in an Article 15 preceding. Soldiers are typically assigned some sort of manual labor task (i.e. mop and wax floors, clean work areas, mow grass, etc.) for their extra duty. These tasks are not to be performed during the typical duty day (9:00-5:00) but after the duty day ends, hence "extra" duty.*** I knew that this decision would worsen his financial situation but I did not linger on that thought long. I came to the conclusion that Davidson had put his family in the financial hardship that they were in. I also contemplated on how many times I had helped this guy already yet he lied, manipulated and took advantage of those who went out of their way to help him.

I knew Davidson had no money, that he was being separated from the Army rather quickly and knew without a shadow of a doubt that this guy had no plan whatsoever on what he was going to do after the

Army. I tried to talk to Davidson a few times about being proactive and start lining things up like a job, travel, living arrangements. I don't think anything I said to that kid ever really sunk in. He was not a forward thinker and obviously did not have his priorities in order and his wife was no better. We tried our best to jump in front of any potential issues but fell short of the mark.

After the Brigade Commander had signed off on Davidson's separation papers, we found ourselves in a logistical whirlwind trying to get this guy out of the Army. We had a week and a half to get him to all of his appointments, all of his gear turned in, get him out of his on-post house and on an airplane back to his home state. This proved to be easier said (or typed in this case) than done. Davidson's on-post house was not clean at all. The new carpeting throughout the house looked like it was five years old. Not only were the floors filthy, but the two of them had been smoking inside the house (with a baby in the house) which saturated the house with a putrid cigarette smoke smell. They ended up owing the housing office over $3500 in rent and fees. When they went to go turn in his gear to the Central Issuing Facility (CIF), it turns out that Davidson didn't have almost three quarters of his stuff; over $900 worth of his equipment was gone. When Davidson was asked where his stuff was, he replied with a typical Soldier answer *"Oh, it was stolen Sergeant."* I have no doubt in my mind that Davidson sold his gear just so he could go buy more pills to feed his addiction. ***If a Soldier does have their gear stolen, it is imperative that a police report is filed. A Financial Liability investigation can then be initiated by the command and the Soldier will more than likely not have to pay to replace it. This does not, however, mean that some sort of administrative or punitive action cannot be taken if***

the Soldiers stupidity or ignorance played a factor in the gear being stolen in the first place (i.e. leaving Army gear in the back seat of a car in plain sight). Davidson had no money left. He was completely broke and had no money coming to him in his last paycheck. What little money he was owed, was taken to pay back what he owed the government, which still wasn't enough to cover all his costs that he had racked up. The housing bill was never paid. He had to sign an agreement saying he would pay within 30 days but they will never see that money. Since government housing is privatized, (worst idea ever) the Army cannot intervene and try to collect this money. Instead, the housing office will have to settle for reporting the failure to pay to the credit bureaus.

The final challenge I faced dealing with this inept family came in the final couple of days before their flight. As I previously stated, Davidson was not a forward thinker; both him and his wife seemed incapable of handling issues without putting themselves even further in a hole. With that said, the issue was that Davidson and his wife had their very last appointment on a Monday morning and they were to fly that afternoon. The Housing Office would not clear them from their house the Friday prior nor would there be enough time to do it on that Monday, there was already too much going on, so his appointment to clear his quarters was set for Thursday; four days before his scheduled flight. With no money and severe lack of common sense, Davidson did not plan accordingly nor had the means to secure a temporary living arrangement. Davidson was authorized some money from the Army for food and a hotel room but would not get the money upfront. He would have to pay for everything then be reimbursed afterward. Therein lies the dilemma, Davidson and his family would be without a place to stay for four nights. It is not necessarily my responsibility to ensure that he has a place to stay, however, I could not have his wife and child sleeping on the streets of Hawaii until his flight. I made several phone calls to Schofield Inn and to Army Emergency Relief trying to ensure this family didn't have to sleep on the street. I inquired to how much a room would cost at Schofield for the four nights and if they had any vacancies. Once I had the exact total, I approved an AER grant for the exact cost of the room. ***Soldiers that are being discharged from the service, whether honorably or not, cannot receive an AER loan. An AER grant can be given instead if the situation warrants it.*** Knowing that this money is donated from other generous Soldiers, I was reluctant to go this route but I didn't seem to have another choice. Another potential roadblock was that Davidson didn't have a way to reserve a room either. Davidson had— $84 dollars in his bank account, no credit card and no other way to secure a room. A hotel typically requires that a card of some sort be placed on the account to cover things like phone calls or movies. We all racked our brain trying to figure out how we were going to get them put up for the time needed. I was at a loss because I didn't know what we were going to do if the hotel would not allow them to check in; there was not a plan B. I went to the Battalion Commander and gave her an update on the situation. I also asked her for guidance or help because I was at a loss if we couldn't pull this off. The BC made a couple phone calls and was able to pull a few strings. With the help of her staff, we were able to move Davidson's flight up to Friday; now all we had to do was ensure he had a place to stay for the night. That night, his supervisor (SSG Willis) took him and his family to the hotel to try and get a room. The front desk attendant at the hotel was leery about allowing them to stay without having a card on file. After a very long explanation of the situation and some pleading on his part, SSG Willis was able to talk them into allowing the family to stay without a card on file. I had instructed SFC Wogomon that SSG Willis was to hold onto the cash Davidson had gotten from AER. I didn't want that Soldier getting any more than what was absolutely necessary.

The next Friday morning had many moving pieces. Davidson and his wife had to be in many places that day and finish up in time to get to the airport for their flight. Davidson had a few last appointments that he to attend and his wife had to take their car to the shipping company so it could be shipped back to the states. Of course, there were issues with the car. Another Soldier had to take the wife to the store to get a brake light for the car and then install it for her before the shipping company would accept it. Of course, she wasn't on the registration either; so we had to get in contact with the Brigade lawyers and have them draft a power of attorney as soon as possible before they could head down to Honolulu with the car.

Finally, the time came when Davidson was finished with each of his appointments. The car was at the shipping dock in route to the states and it was time for them to be headed down to the airport for their flight. SFC Wogomon gave the couple another $100 dollars so they would have money for food at their layovers and we were able to give $300 dollars back to AER. Another Soldier got the burden to have to take the family to the airport, but just like that, Davidson was no longer my problem or the Army's problem to worry about.

The Unhappy Couple

Our Armed Forces have seen unrelenting fighting for over a decade in America's longest war in her history. The continuous fighting and our victories abroad have resulted in our failures back home. The family unit has been neglected and our divorce rate is at an all-time high. That leads me into my next story which elaborates on one of my *experiences* dealing with irate wives.

Sergeant Nelson and his wife had a strained relationship. Their arguments and antics seemed to be cyclic; good one week, bad the next. They were a typical couple with typical problems, to include money. Although they were not having money trouble, I found it ironic that things were good between them when payday rolled around. Nelson's wife didn't work; instead, she stayed home with their two children which wasn't helping her piece of mind either. As soon as Nelson would get home, his wife was ready for a much needed break and wanted to get out of the house. There were several points of contention between the two of them but they always seemed to work it out. The other issue they both had was that both of them didn't deal with their negative situations too well. Their arguments and "punishments" towards one another were, at times, outright childish.

Mrs. Nelson was no stranger to the Army. She volunteered with our Family Readiness Group (FRG) program on a regular basis and I would meet with her and the FRG leader on a monthly basis to plan our upcoming FRG events. When their arguments started getting bad, Mrs. Nelson would call SFC Wogomon or me and tell us what her husband had done and what he had said. Each time she called, her explanations of events that transpired were never anything illegal, just not very husband like. Nelson would threaten to leave and take the kids, threaten to kick her out of the house, he took her phone one time, he blocked her car with his and wouldn't move it so she could leave, he locked her out of the house when she went to go stay with a friend one time, and the list goes on and on. She was trying to use SFC Wogomon and I to get her way with her husband.

SFC Wogomon and I were not too concerned about most of the stories that she came to us with. Locking her out and blocking her car is, however, not ok, so SFC Wogomon got a hold of Nelson and told him that he had to let her in the house and had to allow her to leave if she wanted to.

A few weeks later, I took leave and went to Texas to visit my soon to be wife. This was my first time in Texas and the first opportunity to meet some of my future wife's friends so we had planned some visits while I was in town. One day, we are on our way to visit one of her friends, Brittany, who lived in Erin's old neighborhood. This day stands out so vividly because as we were pulling into the neighborhood, Erin's oldest daughter called. She started with the normal pleasantries but was beating around the bush for some reason. As soon as we pulled up in front of Brittany's house, we hear *"Mom, I'm pregnant."* Erin was so excited! After we got off the phone with her daughter, we walked in and I met Brittany and her kids for the first time. The visit was going very well; Brittany had made a bunch of snacks which were amazing! It makes me hungry just thinking about it. The second reason this day is still so vivid to me is because of what happens next; Mrs. Nelson called.

I stepped onto the back porch, where Brittany's two little dogs were, and answered the phone. Mrs. Nelson was on the other line extremely upset. The two of them had just gotten into a really big fight and she said that she had had enough and wanted out of their relationship. She was calling me, sobbing no less, to inquire about legal assistance that Schofield provided wives and where she could turn to for help with her situation. To put this into perspective, I'm in Texas for the first time, at the house of one of Erin's friends for the first time, we just learned that Erin's oldest was pregnant, yet I'm outside with the two dogs giving advice to and angry and upset wife. Really!?!?! I probably spent 20 minutes on the phone with that woman listening to her continuously complain about how Nelson was acting and how she didn't want to stay with him anymore. I finally got her calmed down and explained what the process typically entails when going through a divorce and what the intermediary steps would be to get her started down the path she said she wanted to go. Afterward, I walked back in, apologized for the interruption and we had a very nice visit.

Once I got back to Hawaii, I called both of them into the office to discuss their behavior. I asked the Brigade Chaplain to come over and sit in on the conversation and provide insight or helpful advice that they could utilize to help their relationship. The four of us were in my office and I got maybe two words in before the Chaplain stepped in and interrupted. *This guy tells me to step out, OF MY OFFICE,* and proceeds to have a couples therapy session with the door closed. I was sitting outside my own damn office with an enormous task list to accomplish yet forced to wait while this Chaplain talks to them. Don't get me wrong, I was glad that they were getting some much needed help, but he could have at least taken them back to his office if he didn't want me to be a part of the discussion.

The good news is that these two are still together. Their childish behavior when they argue still shows up from time to time but has gotten a lot better. Their money situation also improved; Nelson was soon promoted to the rank of Staff Sergeant (SSG/E6) and his wife decided to join the military. She was actually in Basic Training at the time I started writing this book. I wish them the best.

I knew that stepping into the role of Commander meant that I was responsible for the Soldiers *AND* their families . . . I just didn't think I would become a counselor and get that deeply involved. I've had many Soldiers come into my office and talk about their home life and the issues they were having with their significant other. After I would talk to them a little about certain things they could do to improve their relationship, I would always provide them with three things; 1. The book *"Sex Begins in the Kitchen"* 2. The phone number to the chaplain and 3. The number to the Military Family Life Consultant (MFLC). All of which are great resources that will help mend and strengthen any relationship, as long as you put in the effort to fix it.

Drunk on Duty

This next story discusses the actions and misguided decisions of Specialist (SPC) Daniels. I started dealing with issues surrounding Daniels since I initially took command in. Daniels was not always a SPC; he had achieved the rank of SGT before he was demoted and we will get to the WHY later in the story.

SGT Daniels worked at the Schofield Barracks police station as one of the Desk Sergeants. Although he put in most of his efforts in doing his job, Daniels was not a very good Desk Sergeant. In fact, he was the worst one that worked there. Daniels had not proven that he possessed the capability or institutional knowledge needed to operate without supervision. The Senior Desk Sergeant worked many shifts alongside Daniels to ensure he didn't mess up. Daniels was also not a very good Sergeant. He often failed to conduct his duties as a leader and was counseled several times on what he was supposed to do for his Soldiers. All in all, he was not dependable, not self-driven nor motivated to excel.

Daniels' home life was also not very positive. Daniels had recently married one of the Privates from a sister unit. Daniels had previously been in the same unit as his wife which is where they met. ___NCOs should not be fraternizing with Privates! Leaders must maintain their situational awareness within their unit and ensure that their junior Soldiers are protected.___ These two fought like cats and dogs. Daniels' supervisors and even SFC Wogomon had to go over to their residence several times for domestic related issues. The police were even called a few times due to the intense volume their arguments achieved. The main problem was a significant personality conflict between the two. Daniels was a few years older than his wife and didn't like to go out much. She, on the other hand, was young and wanted to go out partying on a regular basis. They still remained together and tried to work through their issues. Later, his wife came down on orders to go to another duty station state side. Daniels had to stay on island due to his legal issues that were still pending.

Only a few days after I took command, the Senior Desk Sergeant, SSG Craft, came into my office to talk about Daniels. *"Sir, I would like you to command direct Daniels to ASAP."* I look back at him and inquire the reason. Craft started telling about an incident that had occurred a couple of months prior to me taking over as the commander. Daniels, along with other Soldiers and Department of the Army Civilian Police (DACP), were doing some training on the Intoxilyzer. As the name indicates, this is a machine that MPs and DACP's use at the police station that measures the amount of alcohol in someone's system. After the subject blows, the Intoxilyzer will give a digital printout of the subjects Blood Alcohol Level that is admissible in a court of law. A couple of days after the training, a few of the students approach Craft and tell him that Daniels blew over the legal limit while they were conducting their training. This guy even rode his motorcycle into work that day. Stupid!! The previous command team made Daniels self-enroll into ASAP. ***If a Soldier self-enrolls into the ASAP program, they can self disenroll out of the program whenever they want to.*** This is exactly what Daniels had done. This was also the catalyst for SSG Craft to come ask me to put him back in it. I asked SSG Craft for the Intoxilyzer print out and any counseling statements regarding this issue. Craft replies back with *"We don't have any, sir."* I looked at SSG Craft with confusion and disbelief, wondering how something like that could not be documented. Given the information, or lack thereof, I decided not to command refer Daniels to ASAP. Everything that Craft had just explained was hearsay and there was no documented evidence that supported a decision for me to honor his request. I felt this would be viewed as an unwarranted and illegal punishment towards Daniels that, oh by the way, occurred two months before I took command. The previous command team did not take the appropriate actions in this case and Daniels' immediate supervisors failed him.

Months had gone by before any serious issue with Daniels had come up. As mentioned before, there were the domestic issues that sprung up and the hardships in his marriage were no secret. He was still complaining about his work environment and that he didn't like working on the Desk; nothing too serious, however, was going on that would raise a caution flag or was cause for concern. Well, one day SSG Craft comes into the office and tells me that Daniels wants to use my open door policy. ***Every commander at every level within the service will have an open door policy. This is a common policy that a Soldier can take advantage of if they feel that their immediate supervisors have failed them or it is in regards to their supervisor.*** I invited Daniels to come in, have a seat and tell me what's on his mind. Daniels started opening up a little bit about his drinking issues. *"Well, how much do you drink?"* I ask. He replies *"Oh sir, I don't know. I don't drink that much."* I actively listened to him explain how much he usually drinks but he starts beating around the bush. I tell him *"Let's take a different approach. How much alcohol do you usually consume a* *day or in a week?"* I get out my pen and sticky note pad and write down what he tells me so I can add it all up. He goes on to tell me he typically bought a 24 pack of beer and a fifth of hard liquor each weekend and consume the entire quantity over the period of only a couple of days. That means this guy was consuming 96 beers and 4 bottles of hard liquor in a one month time frame. OMG!! I explained to him that, in my opinion, that this was a very excessive amount of alcohol for any one person to be drinking. I decided to go ahead and command refer him to the ASAP program. This would give him the opportunity to get the help that he needed and that the appointments would be during the duty day, not on his time off. I shared a couple of personal stories with him in an attempt to mitigate his feelings of loneliness or that he was the only that has gone through rough points in their life. After Daniels and his supervisor left my office, I went ahead and filled out the command referral paperwork to get him over to ASAP. Daniels went a couple days later to meet his counselor and start treatment. The initial Rehabilitative Team Meeting (RTM) with the counselor, Daniels, SFC Wogomon and I was scheduled later on into the next week. As far as his work responsibilities go, he had not demonstrated any degradation in his already lacking abilities so I decided to let him continue performing his law enforcement duties. That is a decision I wish I could take back.

A woman walks into the Schofield Barracks Police station one early afternoon with a very irate and irritated attitude. This woman was upset because she was affected in a negative way when an MP executed their duty; a speeding ticket, a monetary fine of some sort, who knows. These complaints are common but must still be addressed professionally and courteously. This woman was inconsolable. Daniels just so happened to be working at the Desk at that time. He attempted to talk to the woman but she wasn't having any of it. Daniels called back to the Master Sergeant (MSG) in his office and briefly explains what's going on. The MSG told Daniels to bring the irate woman back to his office so he can talk to her and attempt to calm her down. Daniels complied and escorted the woman back to MSG's office. The woman, shaking, huffing and puffing out of frustration, doesn't say anything until Daniels leaves the room. *"Oh HELL NO, THIS IS SOME BULLSHIT!! THIS WHOLE DAMN PLACE IS FUCKED UP!! YOU CANT SMELL HIM?* (referring to SGT Daniels) *HE SMELLS LIKE A BREWERY!!* (Insinuating and accusing Daniels of smelling like alcohol)." The woman, now even more upset than when she started, turns around and storms out of the MSG's office. He runs after her and starts to plea with the woman to talk with him about her issues and assures her that Daniels will be dealt with appropriately. Finally, the MSG was able to calm the woman down and rectify her initial issues; now he had to focus on Daniels.

The MSG pulls Daniels back to his office and attempted to smell his breath and clothes. The MSG then calls me to tell me about what happened then asked for my permission to make Daniels blow on the Intoxilyzer (***A command directed breathalyzer***). I gave my consent but when they ordered Daniels to blow, he refused. After the refusal, I directed the MSG to have Daniels transported to Tripler Army Medical Center and have his blood drawn. As instructed, Daniels' supervisors escorted him to Honolulu but was not able to be seen right away. They arrived at Tripler about 5:00 pm but Daniels' blood wasn't drawn until around 8:00 pm. When we got the results, Daniels had a Blood Alcohol Content (BAC) of 0.17. So let's put this situation into perspective; Daniels reports for work around 1:00 pm that afternoon. The woman didn't smell the alcohol on him until roughly 4:00 pm and his blood wasn't drawn until approximately 8:00 pm. So at 8:00 pm, the Soldier's BAC was over twice the legal limit for him to operate a motor vehicle. One can only imagine his BAC when he showed up for work at 1:00. From 1:00 pm to 4:00 pm, Daniels was responsible for the safety and welfare of over 94,000 Soldiers, civilians and the Military Police Patrols on shift yet was severely intoxicated the entire time.

Daniels was arrested by the same people that he works with on a regular basis. He was charged with Drunk on Duty and Operating a Vehicle Under the Influence of an Intoxicant (OVUII). Daniels was relieved of all Military Police duties and removed from the MP Desk. SGT Daniels was administratively flagged and we initiated the paperwork needed for him to receive a Field Grade Article 15.

The next week, we attended the RTM that was previously scheduled with his counselor. At the RTM, I was not a very nice person. I lit into that Soldier without mercy or regard for the company that was in the room hearing what I had to say. I gave him a piece of mind that I hope he never forgets.

To put this even further into perspective; SGT Daniels rode his motorcycle, *to work,* while drunk to participate in breathalyzer training almost a year before this incident. Daniels disenrolls himself from the ASAP program. Daniels comes into my office and basically says that he drinks like a fish so I do what I can to help him out. And now, Drunk on Duty, twice!? After much reflection on the entire sequence of events, I could not trust this Soldier to make the right decisions. I also was concerned that this *Sergeant* would eventually lead

Soldiers again yet has proven on more than one occasion that he makes very bad decisions. It was time for Daniels to leave the Army.

Another interesting development to this case was that while we were compiling his Article 15 packet, the counseling statement and the Intoxilyzer print out from the first incident surfaced. The previous command had evidence for his first incident and failed to do anything about; furthermore, it seems as if they tried to cover it up.

SGT Daniels was given the Field Grade Article 15 by the Battalion Commander for the charge of Drunk on Duty. The OVUII charge did not hold up since Daniels was not administered the breathalyzer right after exiting his vehicle; therefore, no one could prove that he didn't start drinking on breaks or in an area where no one saw him after he got to work. Daniels was demoted to the rank of Specialist (SPC), had his money taken from him and put on extra duty for 30 days.

I initiated the separation process for to remove SPC Daniels from the Army. When I brought him into the office to inform him of my decision, he said that he wanted to separation board to hear his case. ***A Soldier who is being chaptered/separated from the military and has more than TEN years in service has the right to a Separation Board. The board will determine whether or not justification exists that would warrant the retention of the Soldier of whether their characterization of service (honorable, general, other than honorable) should be changed from the initial recommendations of the Commander.*** Given the severity of Daniels' actions, that they occurred on more than one occasion and that he was going to fight the separation, I characterized his service as Other Than Honorable (OTH). This meant that Daniels would not be eligible for a federal job, would not receive any benefits from the V.A. or be able to get employment with federal contractors hired by the military to work overseas in combat areas. The approval authority for an OTH separation is the first General Officer in my chain of command.

Daniels' request of the Separation Board was not the only method he tried to use to change his fate; he got his ASAP counselor involved. In a few conversations with this counselor, Dr. B had expressed his desire to have Daniels separated under a different chapter; chapter 9. ___*A*___ ___*Chapter 9 separation is for an ASAP failure.*___ Separation under this chapter allows a Soldier to continue getting help with alcoholism from the V.A. after they depart the military.

The strange part about this though is that after my refusal to change the chapter from a Chapter 14—Misconduct, Daniels brought in discharge paperwork from ASAP stating that the he had successfully completed the program. WHAT!?!? This memo was very unprofessional though, it had Daniels' name on it in one place but then another Soldiers name somewhere else. The point of contact was the actual director of ASAP, who hadn't seen a patient in years after he took his leadership position. Everything about this paperwork and the timing that he was bringing it to me seemed very shady. ___*Only the commander*___ ___*that directed a Soldier go to ASAP can release them from the*___ ___*program.*___ I was not willing to do this. SFC Wogomon, Daniels and I had a final meeting with Dr. B at his request. When we got there, Dr. B started talking to us about the ASAP failure chapter (Chapter 9). He also starts offering up his opinion on how I should handle this particular case there in front of the Soldier. I was not very appreciative at all about the situation and environment that Dr. B had just created. I told Daniels to step outside and wait. I was not about to start discussing my thoughts on the matter in front of him nor explain myself while he was in the room. After Daniels walked out, I rebutted Dr B's previous comments about ASAP failure with the faulty and unprofessional paperwork that he had signed saying Daniels was a success and gave the Soldier all high marks. I let Dr. B know that Daniels would remain in the ASAP program until he is out of the military, that I would not change his chapter type and I would not discuss it anymore in the future.

When we pushed Daniels' separation packet up to our higher headquarters, we learned that the Brigade Commander had altered my recommendation and changed his service characterization to a "General Discharge." This meant that Daniels would still be able to receive some benefits from the V.A. but it also meant that an extra level of bureaucracy (red tape) would be eliminated. ***The Brigade Commander is the separation authority for discharges with a service characterization of "General."***

Daniels was still not satisfied with the characterization being "General" and still pushed forward with his request to have a Separation Board hear his case. The Brigade Commander honored his request and a date was set to hear the Daniels' case. At his board, Daniels tried to enter his matters of defense in an attempt to sway the board members to vote favorably on his behalf. A few other Soldiers, to include SFC Wogomon, also testified at the board. The board members did not change his characterization of service nor did they allow him to remain in the military. With that, SPC Daniels is now Mr. Daniels and no longer serves in the armed services.

* *The first supporting document is a copy of Daniels BAC report from the hospital. The second document is a DA Form 4856—Counselling Form that Davis received from his supervisor after his arrest.* *

DEPARTMENT OF DEFENSE
ARMED FORCES MEDICAL EXAMINER SYSTEM
115 PURPLE HEART DRIVE
DOVER AFB, DE 19902-5051

REPLY TO
ATTENTION OF

MCMR-MET

TO:

TRIPLER AMC
1 JARRETT WHITE RD
ATTN: COMMANDING OFFICER
TRIPLER AMC, HI 96859

<u>PATIENT IDENTIFICATION</u>

Name Daniels   SSAN

Toxicology Accession #:
Date Report Generated: 2012

CONSULTATION REPORT ON CONTRIBUTOR MATERIAL

AFMES DIAGNOSIS   REPORT OF TOXICOLOGICAL EXAMINATION

Condition of Specimens: GOOD
Date of Incident: 2012   Date Received: 2012

ETHANOL: The **BLOOD** contained 170 mg/dL of ethanol. Ethanol was identified and quantitated by headspace gas chromatography at a limit of quantitation of 20 mg/dL.

THOMAS Z. BOSY, PhD
CDR, MSC, USN
Certifying Scientist, Forensic Toxicology Laboratory
Armed Forces Medical Examiner System

BARRY LEVINE, PhD, DABFT
Director, Forensic Toxicology Laboratory
Armed Forces Medical Examiner System

DEVELOPMENTAL COUNSELING FORM
For use of this form, see FM 6-22; the proponent agency is TRADOC

DATA REQUIRED BY THE PRIVACY ACT OF 1974

PART I - ADMINISTRATIVE DATA

Name (Last, First, MI)	Rank/Grade	Date of Counseling
Daniels	SGT/E-5	12

Organization	Name and Title of Counselor
13th Military Police Detachment Schofield Barracks, Hawaii	SSG ████ Operatrions Sergeant Willis

PART II - BACKGROUND INFORMATION

Purpose of Counseling: (Leader states the reason for the counseling, e.g. Performance/Professional or Event-Oriented counseling, and includes the leader's facts and observations prior to the counseling.)

Event-Oriented Counseling-

Purpose of this counseling is to discuss the events that took place on ████ 2012, which caused you to be titled with violation of Article #111 (Drunken Driving) and Article # 112 (Drunk on Duty) UCMJ.

PART III - SUMMARY OF COUNSELING
Complete this section during or immediately subsequent to counseling.

Key Points of Discussion:

SGT ████, at 1600 on 2012 ████, MSG ████ was notified that you were possibly drunk on duty at Building # 3010(SB). Investigation by T-7 ████, Nighthawk-7 ████, and DS6 ████ revealed that you drove your 2012 Infiniti ████ to the Schofield Barracks PMO and assumed Desk Sergeant duties at 1300 on 2012 ████. You submitted to a PBT which resulted in a 0.174 BRAC. You elected to take a blood test and not the Intoxilyzer. SSG ████ and SSG ████ then transported you to Tripler Army Medical Center where you relinquished a blood test. You were then transported back to the SB Police Station where you were advised of your legal rights, which you invoked. You were then further processed and released to SFC Wogomon on a DD Form 2708. You were titled with violation of Article #111 (Drunken Driving) and Article # 112 (Drunk on Duty) UCMJ. You were also Command Referred into the Army Substance Abuse Program by CPT Hepler IAW Army Regulation 600-85 (The Army Substance Abuse Program). When you were enrolled into ASAP you signed the enrollment counseling which stated that you would not drink any alcohol while in ASAP. You have verbally admitted that you violated this while at your wife's birthday dinner. SGT ████, since working at AO-North Desk this is your second alcohol related incident. Working on the Desk is a stressful and highly intensive duty which includes making multiple decisions which affect the health and welfare of everyone living or working in the AO-North Communities. While working in this position it is imperative that you are focused on the mission at hand, you have proven that you cannot perform this duty. On 2012 ████, you were relieved of your duties as Desk Sergeant and are now assigned to work in Operations pending UCMJ action. Your DEROS will also be adjusted, ensure your wife is aware that you will not PCS with her to Ft. ████ and do not ship any CIF gear that you would normally be able to PCS with. While working in Operations you will report to myself everyday for physical training no later than 0620 at the CTA. On Monday and Friday you will wear your green BN t-shirt for physical training. Your responsibilities while assigned to Operations will be to assist me with tracking all documents turned into the Detachment and any other tasking that the Detachment is given. You will give me a copy of all appointments that you have so I can ensure you make all of them. If you have any questions or concerns do not hesitate to call me.

This counseling is furnished to you not as a punitive measure, but as an administrative measure to stress that if this conduct continues, action may be initiated to seperate you from the Army under AR 635-200 Chapter 4,5,9,11,13,14, or 18. Continuation of this pattern of misconduct for which you are specifically being counseled may warrant seperation under Chapter 14. If you are involuntarily seperated, you could recieve an Honorable discharge, General discharge, or Other Than Honorable discharge. If you recieve an Honorable discharge you will qualify for most benefits resulting from military service. An Involuntary Honorable discharge, however, will be disqualifying from reenlistment and may disqualify you from receiving transitional benefits (e.g. commissary, health benefits) and Post 9-11 G.I. Bill or Montgomery G.I. Bill. If you receive a General discharge, you will not recieve money for educational purposes and any money already contributed for educational purposes is nonrefundable.

OTHER INSTRUCTIONS

This form will be destroyed upon reassignment (other than rehabilitative transfers), separation at ETS, or upon retirement. For separation requirements and notification of loss of benefits/consequences see local directives and AR 635-200.

DA FORM 4856, AUG 2010   PREVIOUS EDITIONS ARE OBSOLETE   APD PE v1.00ES

Immoral Dog Handler

This next story is about SSG Holman. Holman was a Military Working Dog handler by trade and one of the more experienced handlers within the kennel. SSG Holman was good at being a dog handler and he knew it. SSG Holman was cocky and very arrogant but I never would have guessed he had such a level of immorality and selfishness in him.

It all started when an Animal Control Officer responded to a Domestic Disturbance at a residence on Schofield Barracks. A teenager had been bitten in the face and hand by a Soldiers one year old Belgian Malinois *(pronounced Mal - en - wa)*. The owner of the dog was friends with the father of the kid that was bitten. The reports say that the kid (17 years old) was trying to play with the dog while it was eating. The kid was down on all fours and put his face right up to the dogs while it was eating. As most young male dogs do when you're in its face and their eating, it looked up and bit him. I would classify this as a provoked bite; not the dogs fault. When the Animal Control Officer arrived, the dog owner explained what had happened; the officer took photos of the boy's wounds then informs the owner that the dog has to be confiscated. The owner was not happy at all about the course of action but the Animal Control Officer told him that it was a Schofield Barracks policy and the dog had to be put down. The owner reluctantly relinquished his dog and the Animal Control Officer left.

Schofield Barracks Police Station procedure for an animal that is confiscated or captured is to put it in a temporary holding area beside the Station. Once all the paperwork is completed, the Animal Control Officer will take the confiscated or captured animals to the Honolulu Humane Society for adoption or destruction.

As the K9 perpetrator was waiting there on *death row* to be taken to the Humane Society, MSG Tuttle (a prior dog handler himself) just so happened to walk by and see the dog in the cage. He goes back to the kennel (*which is located right beside the police station*) and tells the Kennel Master and some of the other handlers what he saw, to include SSG Holman. They all stroll over to look at the dog. The handlers were already sympathetic to the dog because he looked like half the dogs that were in the kennel already. ***The military uses only a few breeds of dogs for official purposes. The most common breeds, but not limited to, are German Shepherds and Belgian Malinois'. I also had two Labs and a Weimaraner in the kennel at this particular time.*** MWD handlers are very comfortable and used to working with these breeds of dogs and are very aware of their capabilities and future health issues that could develop.

SSG Holman was the one who was apparently affected the most by this situation. The Kennel Master and SSG Holman went inside the Police Station to talk with the Animal Control Officer about the dog and elaborated on their intent to not have this dog put down. They all collaborated and agreed that SSG Holman and the Kennel Master would follow the Animal Control Officer to the Humane Society. Once they were in Honolulu, the Animal Control Officer releases the dog into custody of the Humane Society knowing the dog is *supposed* to be destroyed. Once the Animal Control Officer left, the Kennel Master and SSG Holman start going to work.

They start giving the Humane Society employees a brief oral résumé of what they do and how than can ensure this dog can be rehabilitated. They also explained the circumstances around the incident and how the dog was provoked. After hearing their arguments, the Humane Society employees agreed with their position on the matter. Instead of destroying the dog like they were supposed to, they adopted it out to SSG Holman. The dog lives.

Here's the problem; the owner calls down to the Humane Society to find out if his dog had been put down. He was deceptive at first and told the Humane Society that his dog was "*lost*" instead of telling the truth. The Humane Society told him that they didn't have his dog and that someone had adopted it out. As you would imagine, the dog owner was infuriated. He was told by a Law Enforcement Official that he had to relinquish his dog and the dog was to be destroyed. From his point of view, his very expensive dog was stolen from him and then given to someone else. The other dilemma was the pretense under which the Humane Society released the dog in the first place; they were under the impression that the dog would be incorporated into the Army Military Working Dog program and used for official purposes, not serve as someone's pet.

The dog owner started digging into what exactly happened to his dog and why the police had lied to him. The Humane Society would not release personal information to the original owner, but through hostile conversation, the Humane Society let slip that the person that adopted the dog worked with Military Working Dogs. Naturally, the original dog owner went to the Police Station to try and find out who took his dog. Unfortunately, there was no record of this guy's dog being dropped off at the Humane Society. The Animal Control Officer did not follow the proper procedures and failed to obtain the necessary paperwork form the Humane Society showing a proper chain of custody for the animal. After the dog owner explains the situation to the MP at the Desk, that MP calls SSG Willis.

SSG Willis meets with the dog owner to get the particulars surrounding the situation. SSG Willis gets SFC Wogomon involved and they both start piecing this whole story together. Once SFC Wogomon tells me what was going on, I headed over to the Brigade legal office to get some legal advice. I explain the situation to the lawyer:

- *The owner was told his dog had to be confiscated and destroyed.*
- *The owner didn't want to give the dog up.*
- *The Kennel Master and SSG Holman intervened in the process.*
- *SSG Holman had valid adoption paperwork from the Humane Society and legally adopted the dog.*
- *The original owner either wanted his dog back or have the dog destroyed.*

The lawyer and I had a teleconference with the Humane Society and quickly brought them up to speed on the situation. The representative that we spoke to didn't have knowledge of this particular incident but did state that it is not in their policies to automatically put down a dog just because it bit someone. The rep went on to say that if they knew the bite was provoked, they would consider adopting the dog out. After we hung up, the Brigade lawyer said that there was nothing we could do to SSG Holman. He hadn't violated any articles within the Uniform Code of Military Justice (UCMJ) and legally adopted the dog. Although I thought SSG Holman was an asshole for his actions, I didn't have a legal leg to stand on. Frustrating!! SSG Holman was not willing to give the dog back either.

The original dog owner was still persistent. After failing to get his dog back on his own, he turned to the Inspector General (IG). *__A Soldier can take their issue(s) to the IG office if they feel that have been treated unjustly or unfairly. The Soldiers that work within IG will investigate the allegations and then report their findings to the accuser's chain of command if their investigation proves the allegation to be true. Actions can then be taken to rectify the situation.__* The IG office contacted the Battalion Command Sergeant Major and started asking their questions. SFC Wogomon had to provide all of the documentation showing where SSG Holman adopted the dog legally. IG told the dog owner that they could not assist him since SSG Holman didn't violate the law. The Soldier's only recourse at this point was to file a civil suit against SSG Holman or the Humane Society to try and get his dog back. Another possible course of action would be to write his Congressman. *__Every Soldier has the right to write to their Congressman to inform them of an injustice or unfair treatment they might be receiving that isn't being handled by their chain of command to a satisfactory level. If warranted, the Congressman's office can initiate an inquiry into the allegations. A Congressional Inquiry must be formally investigated and answered, in writing, within a timely manner by the accuser's chain of command.__*

The immorality surrounding the issue is that the dog owner was forced to give up his dog by a Law Enforcement Officer and told that the dog was to be put down. The Kennel Master and SSG Holman used their position, rank and authority to manipulate the Humane Society into allowing the dog to be adopted out instead of putting it down. SSG Holman was not even willing to pay the original owner for this dog. The original owner was manipulated by the police that ultimately led to SSG Holman stealing this dog. Legal documentation or not is irrelevant, at least to me.

The dog still remains with SSG Holman. The original owner had not filed a suit against him, at least at the time I was writing this book. I believe the highest level of fault lies with the Animal Control Officer and the Humane Society for not following through with destroying the dog. Although I don't want harm to come to the dog, they violated the official process by not doing what they were supposed to. This whole situation negatively reflects on the MPs and the Military Working Dog section in a very bad way and inadvertently victimizes the original dog owner. Shame on SSG Holman!!

Toxic Leadership

Toxic Leadership has no place within the armed forces or any other professional workplace. Toxic Leadership breeds low morale, decreases proficiency and work performance. No one wants to work for a toxic leader!

This next story tells a tale of just that; toxic leadership. The transgressor highlighted in the following words is SSG Michaels. SSG Michaels was a Military Working Dog handler and for a brief while, the second in charge of the Schofield Barracks Kennel; his position fell right below that of the Kennel Master on the hierarchy of the kennel leadership.

Before I took Command of the 13th Military Police Detachment, I worked within the Operations section in the Brigade. While in the Brigade, I was able to develop a few professional business relationships with other supporting sections within the Brigade. One such relationship was with SFC Madison, the Brigade Equal Opportunity Advisor.

I was holding my weekly Detachment training meeting in my conference room when the door opened and familiar face peered through the crack; it was SFC Madison. She apologized for her interruption but said *"I need to talk to you."* I ask *"can it wait?"* *"It really can't"* she replies. I let SFC Wogomon finish up the meeting in my absence and headed back to my office.

SFC Madison was waiting there with two of my female military working dog handlers, both E-5/sergeants in rank. These two were very upset and went to SFC Madison to file a formal complaint against

SSG Michaels. Out of courtesy, SFC Madison brought them to me instead before filing the complaint, providing me an opportunity to handle the situation before it was brought to the attention of the Brigade Commander. SFC Madison quickly explained some of the story while the two dog handlers were waiting outside the office. I asked them to come on in so I could hear their issues first hand. By this time, SFC Wogomon had concluded the training meeting and came into the office to hear all that was being said.

These two females were very distraught, upset and just all around pissed. They started elaborating on the unfair treatment that they both were receiving and the poor quality of life that fostered within the kennel; they hated coming to work each day. The biggest and most prevalent complaint they had was that SSG Michaels was a sexist and displayed discriminatory, hostile, unfair and inappropriate behavior towards them yet treated the guys within the kennel much differently. One of the females even told me that her quality of life within the kennel was so bad that it was affecting her physically, that her menstruation cycle had been become irregular and was seeing a doctor. They told me about incidents of:

Sexual Harassment—On more than one occasion, SSG Michaels had made sexually suggestive comments and unwanted advances towards them. They told him that his comments were unappreciated and to stop but they never did file a complaint at the time of the incident. ___It is important to encourage your subordinates to always report sexual harassment to you or the proper reporting agency. A person that sexually harasses one person will continue to harass others until they are caught.___

Favoritism—SSG Michaels displayed many levels of favoritism towards the male Soldiers that he did not reciprocate to the females. SSG Michaels would invite Soldiers to his house but not open the invitation up to the entire kennel. He would hang out with some of the lower enlisted guys on a regular basis.

Lack of Communication

Unprofessional Behavior / Unprofessional Communication—SSG Michaels on several occasions would yell, curse and scream at the subordinates within the kennel. He would become publically irate with some of the lower enlisted Soldiers; some of which he was hanging out with just a few days prior. The Kennel Master even described an incident where he had to correct SSG Michaels because of the way he was yelling at a Soldier.

Fairness of the Schedule—The females described how they were always being put on the schedule to work Law Enforcement yet most of the male handlers were not.

Spreading rumors—SSG Michaels made an inappropriate comment about why one of the females, who was married at the time, was friends with a guy but their "friendship" had some benefits. This comment turned into a rumor that spread through the kennel and caused hardship between her and her husband.

Personal information not kept in confidentiality—While in front of the group at the kennel, one of the females medical issue was brought up without her permission to use as an example. She was embarrassed and humiliated in front of all of her peers.

Unrealistic expectations—Dog handlers are required to maintain their training hours throughout the month in order to remain certified on the dog. The two females were having difficulty maintaining this requirement because they were always being put onto the schedule to work Law Enforcement. SSG Michaels would still meticulously scrutinize their training records and then fuss at them, telling them they had to make up those training hours yet did not provide any way for them to accomplish this.

After they gave me the rundown of all that they had experienced and were going through while being assigned to the kennel, I ask them if they would afford me the opportunity to fix the situation at my level. I explained that they had every right to be upset and to file a complaint with SFC Madison if they wanted to. They both agreed to let me deal with it, SFC Madison was satisfied with that and they all dismissed themselves. SFC Wogomon and I deliberated for a few minutes trying to wrap our heads around what had just happened.

I called another working dog handler to my office, SSG Wilkinson. I had confidence that he would not feed me a bunch of bullshit and give me a straight forward answer. I didn't tell him about the two females that came into the office nor did I explain the formal accusations that had been made. I simply asked him some questions about SSG Michaels and for him to talk about the things that he had observed while he had been down in the kennel. *This is something I would have done differently if I had to do it over again.* **_I should have_** *initiated a Commanders Inquiry into the incident and let the "process" take its course. By asking my own questions, I divested myself of my authority to adjudicate any punitive actions if I uncovered more than what the two girls had just told me. Leaders, if you are brought information that possibly violates the articles of the UCMJ, inform JAG, appoint an Investigating Officer and initiate a 15-6 or Commanders Inquiry. You should not be asking any questions into the matter at all.*

Wilkinson had confirmed much of what the two females had told me earlier. He did not witness the harassment but told me that SSG Michaels does have favorites. He said SSG Michaels would be very critical to those subordinates that weren't in his little circle. He went on to say SSG Michaels did display a bias towards the females.

After hearing the accusations from the two female working dog handlers and the informal testimony of SSG Wilkinson, I decided that it was time for SSG Michaels to be removed from the kennel. SFC Wogomon agreed with the course of action and went to talk to the acting Battalion Command Sergeant Major. *The Command Sergeant Major is responsible for moving and placing NCOs throughout the unit.* Only he could remove SSG Michaels. The acting CSM agreed with our course of action and told us that he would move SSG Michaels to another unit immediately. I generated a counseling statement for SSG Michaels and a Letter of Concern for the Kennel Master. I still held the Kennel Master at fault as well for being negligent and unaware of the environment that he allowed to foster within the kennel.

I called SSG Michaels and the Kennel Master both into my office, SFC Wogomon was already there. I didn't give SSG Michaels any time to defend himself at all. I briefly discussed the accusations that had been brought against him and told him that he would be removed from the kennel for the safety and morale of the working dog handlers, then issued him his counseling statement. Of course, he was caught off guard and was not happy at all with my decision. He squabbled for a minute and trying to conjure up some excuse that would make me change my mind but his efforts were futile. I dismissed him but told the Kennel Master to remain. I told him that I still held him just as responsible for allowing these kinds of incidences to occur under his watch. I provided him with the Letter of Concern that I had written for him and had him read a professional excerpt that I had, titled "Toxic Leadership."

The next day, SSG Michaels came to me with a memo that he wrote that talked about all the negative incidences and issues that he knew about yet no action was taken. As I read it, I started getting a little upset; not only at him, but the previous command team that was so blind to these issues. I was stunned that SSG Michaels would even bring me something like this. This memo didn't contain any matters of defense on his behalf, instead it talked about all the other stuff that others had gotten away with. This guy was now just "grasping at straws," trying to pull others down with him any way he could. Realizing this, I refused to tear the kennel apart any further by investigating. I did, however, give the memo to the Kennel Master along with a warning; that he needed to tighten up his section and pull his head out of his ass if any one of the statements were true.

SSG Michaels was moved to a new unit that next day and was not allowed back into the kennel from that day forward. The good news is that SSG Michaels performance in his new unit was excellent. His leaders constantly made positive comments about his abilities.

Eventually, SSG Michaels time on the island had come to an end and he was stationed elsewhere. SSG Michaels is now back into another kennel at his new duty assignment. Hopefully, he has learned his lesson.

* The following document is the Letter of Concern that I wrote and issued to the Kennel Master. *

DEPARTMENT OF THE ARMY
13th MILITARY POLICE DETACHMENT
BLDG 765 REILLY AVE
SCHOFIELD BARRACKS, HAWAII 96857

REPLY TO
ATTENTION OF

APTS-MPB-MA   2011

MEMORANDUM FOR SFC ▬▬▬▬▬ (Kennel Master)

SUBJECT: Letter of Concern

1. I am concerned about the morale and welfare of the Soldiers that work within the kennel. I have received reports of many violations of unprofessional conduct, sexual harassment, discrimination, belittling, personal information being publicly disseminated and much more. My concern is that some of these infractions and violations occurred under your direct supervision. Ignorance to the issues is no excuse. Failure to make immediate corrections of unprofessional conduct is unacceptable. Your failure to take action only reinforces the negative behavior and has a direct impact on the morale and welfare of the Soldiers within your section. This will not continue. Leaders within your section will enforce the standards and remain professional in the presence of your Soldiers at all times. All of the leaders within our unit must present a united and professional front if we are to unlock the true potential of those that work for us. We must all understand that we are not only developing Soldiers, but parents and spouses. The manner in which we treat them will inadvertently spill over into a Soldiers home life in a negative way. This is also unacceptable. Any corrective action or disciplinary measures that are taken will be implemented professionally and without bias.

2. Targeting or singling a Soldier out due to poor work performance will not be tolerated. I understand that Leaders must check up on Soldiers and perform audits to ensure accuracy, consistency, and validity. These checks must be fair across the board. If you or the training NCO scrutinizes one set of records, then you must scrutinize all records. If you're going to check camera logs on one person then you must check them for every shift. There must be a system in place where these checks are done regularly and without bias. Counselings will be utilized when a Soldier has made a mistake or had an error in judgment. Immediate spot corrections and written quarterly counselings will be conducted to identify areas of performance that could be improved upon.

3. Soldiers must know that they can trust their leaders and their leaders have their best interests at heart. Toxic leadership will not be tolerated within this unit. Toxic leadership fosters a hostile work environment which will not be tolerated within this unit. Put Soldiers first in all that you do. Identify and correct toxic leadership traits that are displayed by the leaders within your section. You are as much at fault as the leader displaying these negative traits if you allow it to occur. I have already provided you with the professional reading regarding toxic leadership. I encourage you to seek out other useful education material that will hone your leadership skills. Learn from this incident and ensure that these types of infractions do not occur again.

Super Cop

This story is about a young and misguided individual named SPC Thrasher. This kid was quite a piece of work and took his job of being an MP beyond the levels of professionalism and safety. This guy had already been booted out of the Army one time for patterns of misconduct. He wrote and solicited the assistance of his congressman on the matter, which in turn spawned an investigation into his case and ultimately uncovered that SPC Thrashers case was not handled properly by the Army so he was permitted to return to the service. Bad Idea!!

SPC Thrasher did not seem to learn his lesson at all. His conduct, behavior and decisions continue to flirt with and sometimes cross the lines of morality. SPC Thrasher engaged in a contract marriage with another Soldier within my unit. SPC Thrasher had made racist comments to a Private. Ultimately, SPC Thrasher could not follow instructions, be where he was supposed to be on time nor carry himself with integrity or dignity; he was an all-around creep and trouble waiting to happen. With all of that said, none of that is in the following paragraphs.

SPC Thrasher was friends with another Soldier in my unit named SPC Hanson. SPC Hanson, which I will talk about later, is also a piece of work. SPC Hanson has neither common sense nor an ethical or moral bone in his chubby big body. SPC Hanson was one of my traffic accident investigators that worked at the For Shafter Police Station. One night (at about midnight), another Military Police patrolman,

E-5/Sergeant in rank, was sitting in the Burger King parking lot observing an intersection that was notorious for people blowing through the stop signs. The patrolman spotted a vehicle approach the stop sign, does a "rolling stop" and pulled into the Burger King parking lot. The patrolman watches the vehicle pull into a parking stall but the driver doesn't get out and is now curious. About three minutes go by and the driver hasn't moved. The patrolman moves his vehicle into a parking stall that is one back and one over from the vehicle he had been observing, still nothing; the driver just sat there. After about ten minutes, the driver got out of his car and walked towards the patrol car. It is SPC Thrasher in some jeans and a hoodie. The patrolman says *"May I help you?"* SPC Thrasher pulls out and flashes a badge and tells the patrolman that he is an MP also and works the MP Desk at Fort Shafter. SPC Thrasher says in a joking fashion *"I was waiting for you to fall asleep so I could catch you and report you to your Patrol Supervisor"* then chuckles about his comment. The funny part about this portion of the story is that MPs don't get official Police Badges. There are MP Badges out there but they are not for official purposes. SPC Thrasher went and bought one then went parading around and flashing it to people. Moron!! The Sergeant was not too pleased with Thrashers comments but chose not to let the comment bother him. Thrasher says *"I'm waiting for SPC Hanson so I can give him his food. Do you know where he is?* The patrolman told him that SPC Hanson was conducting a traffic stop and asked if he wanted him to call Hanson over the radio. *"No, that's ok. I'll just call him on his cell phone."* Thrasher said. The patrolman goes on to ask *"why are you up at this hour anyway bringing Hanson food?"* Thrasher told him *"I was supposed to bring him food at 9 o'clock but am just now getting* around to it. Besides, I'm just gonna crash on the couch after I get back from DeReussy." "Why are you going down there?" the patrolman asks. "I'm gonna assist with possible DUI's (driving under the influence) and point them out with my badge. I know I can't apprehend anyone but I'll help point them out and if someone gets rowdy, I'll be there to step in and help." The patrolman couldn't do anything but stare at him in disbelief.

A couple of hours later, Thrasher met up with Hanson were both at the 24 hour shoppette there on Fort Shafter. A call came over Hanson's radio that there was a suspicious person around that area. SPC Hanson, being the genius that he is, responds to the call but asks SPC Thrasher to help with the search. And of course, Thrasher was more than willing to assist, while in civilian clothes, and put his nose where it didn't belong. REALLY!?! Hanson jumped into his patrol car and Thrasher jumped into his personal vehicle and headed over to where the suspicious guy was seen last. There are patrol cars and Thrashers car combing a housing area looking for this guy. This was incredibly stupid on Thrashers part!! Luckily, they did not find anyone and the search was called off. But what if Thrasher was the one who spotted that guy? I believe whole heartedly that he would have attempted to apprehend him while flashing that stupid badge. Thrasher had no weapons nor did he have a radio to call for help. Hanson put Thrasher in danger by even asking him to help. Thrasher put himself in danger and they both put the suspect in danger if Thrasher had been the one to find him. I mean seriously, picture that; a guy in regular street clothes try's to stop you on the street while flashing a fake badge in your face. No uniform, nothing indicating he was a law enforcement officer and no gun. Thrasher was a little fella too; he would have gotten his ass handed to him!

Later, Thrasher followed Hanson down to Fort DeReussy like he said he would. While down there, Hanson approached a parked vehicle that had people in it. As he walks up to the car, there's a girl sitting in the driver's seat. Hanson claims to have smelled alcohol on the woman's breath and asks her to step out of the vehicle. As he pulls her out, he notices Thrasher standing about 50 feet away, still in street clothes, watching what was going on. There was also another Department of the Army Civilian Police (DACP) officer there at the time to assist Hanson if needed. As Hanson, starts to conduct a field sobriety test, one of the passengers in the back seat starts haggling Hanson and telling him that he wasn't doing the FST correctly; that he was going to report him to his superiors. As the guy in the back seat continues to give Hanson a hard time, Thrasher walks up to the vehicle and tells the passenger to be quiet and mind his own business. Again, Thrasher's lucky the passenger didn't tell him to go screw himself since he was not in uniform. Thrasher identified himself as an MP and repeated his ultimatum to the passenger to be quite. Hanson looks up *"what are you doing?" "I'm telling the passenger to calm down"* said Thrasher. Hanson didn't seem to see the issue with this and continued to let Thrasher interfere with his scene.

The next day, I was told what had happened and about SPC Thrasher's escapade. I really couldn't quite wrap my head around the story. How could someone be so stupid!?!?! In order to get all the facts involving the incident, I initiated a Commanders Inquiry into the matter. I appointed a Sergeant First Class (SFC/E-7) as the investigating officer and had the Brigade lawyer's type up his appointment orders. We also administratively flagged Thrasher due to his pending investigation.

Once the investigation was concluded, some of the excuses that were given were just as outlandish and almost comical as the original incident. When asked by the investigator why he went to Fort DeReussy in the first place, he responds with *"I go down there to meet women."* What!?!? Readers understand; this place that he's talking about is a *parking lot!* Right across from Fort DeReussy is a federally owned parking lot that is open to the public. Therefore, the Army has joint jurisdiction within the confines of this parking lot. This is where Thrasher is picking up women. I could not help myself but to laugh when I read the findings.

The findings were the other problem that I had. I include the Investigating Officer's findings memo in the supporting documents to this story. In there, he writes that Thrasher did not violate the Army Regulation 600-50 (Standards of Conduct for Department of the Army Personnel) because he didn't actually make contact with the suspicious person. The investigator goes on to write that Thrasher did not act in an official capacity and did not interfere with Hanson's police duties while at the Fort DeReussy parking lot. I did not agree with the findings at all. Although no contact was made with the suspicious person, Thrasher still put his self at risk and did violate the regulation. Furthermore, the minute Thrasher identified himself as an MP to the passengers in the vehicle, he was acting in an official capacity. I was not pleased with the effort that the investigating officer had put in. Given the evidence that had been presented before me and counseling statement from previous incidences with a consultation with the Brigade lawyers, I decided to give SPC Thrasher a Company Grade Article 15. I reduced him in rank to Private First Class (PFC/E3) and gave him Extra Duty for 14 days.

An Inpatient Soldier

This story is about a Specialist (SPC/E4) that violated one written law and a few that are unspoken. The SPC referenced in the words below is SPC Botill. SPC Botill was an eager young Soldier and a relatively decent worker. His impatience and lack of knowledge of inner unit politics, however, would be his down fall.

Before Botill was assigned to my unit, he was assigned to one of my sister Companies within the Battalion. While serving in this other unit, Botill and his leadership were compiling his promotion packet for submission so SPC Botill could be promoted to the rank of Sergeant/E-5. SPC Botill felt that his packet was not being compiled fast enough and took it upon himself to email the Battalion Command Sergeant Major (CSM). The Battalion CSM was deployed at the time along with the entire Headquarters and Headquarters Detachment (HHD). Botill did not afford anyone within his chain of command to help him with his packet. Instead, he wrote directly to the CSM, five positions of enlisted levels of leadership above him. He bypassed his team leader, squad leader, Platoon Sergeant, First Sergeant and the Master Sergeant that was doing the duties of the Battalion CSM in lieu of the CSM. SPC Botill didn't seem to understand the functionality of inner unit politics and burned a lot of bridges.

The CSM wrote the young Soldier back and encouraged him in the future to utilize his chain of command and give them the opportunities to fix the problem before bringing it to his level. The CSM does not, however, ignore Botill's solicitation and orders the

First Sergeant (1SG) from his previous unit and SFC Wogomon to look into the situation and get it fixed. SFC Wogomon and the other 1SG started going through his packet piece by piece. Collectively, they ensured that he had all the items he needed for promotion and even hand carried it over to the Battalion administrative section (S1) to ensure that his packet was expedited through the process.

Soon after Botill's packet was submitted, he was on the road to being promoted. All he had to do was nothing and he would be a Sergeant right now, but his impatience got the better of him. SPC Botill was still not satisfied at the amount of time his packet was taking to be processed so, SPC Botill wrote his Congressman. My boss emailed me the Congressional and asks *"I thought we took care of this?"*

As far as we were concerned, we had done all that we could do in order to get this guy promoted but prudence dictated that we re-verify everything. SFC Wogomon goes back to the S1 office to get his packet. Once the packet was in hand, SFC Wogomon reviewed every document with a fine toothed comb. He wanted to ensure we didn't miss anything and that we could report back to the Congressman that we had put forth every effort that we could.

As SFC Wogomon was going through his packet, he noticed a slight discrepancy with his weapon qualification card. Earlier that week, we received a memo from the officer in charge of the firing range that SPC Botill had fired at. The memo had the names, last four digits of their social security number and their score of all the Soldiers that fired that day. The weapon card that he submitted for his packet stated that he received the score of Expert. The memo we received, however, indicated that SPC Botill didn't even qualify on his weapon. Once SFC Wogomon brought this to my attention, I initiated a Commander Inquiry into the matter and appointed a Sergeant First Class (SFC/E-7) as the Investigating Officer.

The IO discovered that not only did SPC Botill submit a false document, but that he forged an officers and an NCO's name that made it seem like the score had been validated by the both of them. Once the investigation was concluded, SFC Wogomon counseled him and recommended punitive action. Botill was charged with two offenses; submitting a false official record with the intent to deceive, a violation of Article 107 of the UCMJ and forging a signature onto the weapons card, a violation of Article 123 of the UCMJ.

I took SFC Wogomon's recommendation and initiated a Company Grade Article 15 for the two charges above. During my deliberation of the case and evidence, I wasn't quite sure if the Sergeant who said he *didn't* sign the card, really did. We compared the signature on the card to another document that had his signature and it appeared to be a spot on match. With such a similarity between the two signatures, I didn't know if the Sergeant was covering his tracks and throwing Botill "under the bus." After considering everything I had been presented, I found Botill guilty of the Article 107 for submitting a false weapons qualification card. I found him Not Guilty, however, of an Article 123 violation. There was too much similarity between the supposed forged signature and the Soldiers verified signature.

When it came time to dish out his punishment, the main factor that weighed on my mind was that this Soldier lied in order to get promoted to the rank of Sergeant. A Sergeant is looked upon as a leader and is expected to have high morals, ethical standards and good, old fashioned common sense. SPC Botill did not display any of these things by committing this act. Secondly, his score on the weapons card was what gave him the amount of points needed to achieve the next higher rank. A score of "Unqualified" would not have given him the points he needed to be promoted. Given these two circumstances, I decided to send him backwards instead of forward. I reduced him in rank to Private First Class (PFC/E-3), forfeiture of $455 and extra duty for 14 days. Both the forfeiture in pay and extra duty were suspended. ***Suspended punishment from an Article 15 means that the punishment is held over the violators head yet is not carried out. The suspensions can be vacated if the violator gets into trouble again. This means the violator will receive the punishments from the previous Article 15 on top of the punishment they are dealt for their most current indiscretion.*** After I read the Soldiers punishment, he invoked his right to appeal my decision to reduce him in rank. The appeal was sent up to the Battalion Commander but the BC agreed with me and did not overturn my ruling. After the Article 15 proceedings were closed, I talked to Botill for a little bit. He was still unclear why he was getting so much attention and why his packet had been scrutinized so thoroughly. I tried to explain to him that this is what happens when you elevate things to such a high level. I asked him *"why didn't you give your leadership a chance to help you? Senior NCOs get frustrated when they are blindsided and not afforded the opportunity to handle things "in-house" first; when things are taken outside the family."* My statement was an attempt to try and give the Soldier some insight on inner unit politics. Well, he apparently didn't take it that way.

As you could imagine, Botill was not about to go down without a fight. So, he wrote his Congressman, *again.* The complaint this time was that he felt he was being reprised against for talking directly to the CSM down range (deployed in Afghanistan) and for writing his Congressman the first time. When I got the inquiry, I just shook my head and laughed. Within the paragraphs of the congressional inquiry, Botill targets SFC Wogomon and me. Botill took our words out of context and twisted them in his petition to the Congressman that made him out to be a victim rather than a liar.

Although we received two congressional inquiries on the behalf of SPC, now PFC Botill, it did not sway the outcome any different than what I had initially intended it to be. We provided the Congressman's office copies of the investigation that was conducted and the punishment that was dealt. This satisfied the Congressman and this matter was officially closed.

* *The following supporting documents include:*

1. *Botill's letter to his Congressman*
2. *The Congressman's letter ordering an investigation*
3. *Letter from the Congressman back to Botill*
4. *Memorandum from the NCO that ran the range*
5. *The forged weapons card and the Article 15 I gave*

 2011

Botill

Wahiawa, HI 96786
Phone:

Bob Latta & Staff
1045 N. Main Street, Suite 6
Bowling Green, Ohio 43402-1361
Phone: (419)-354-8700

Dear Bob Latta,

I am SPC _____ with the 13th Military Police Detachment, 728th MP Battalion, 8th MP Brigade out of Schofield Barracks, Hawaii. I come to you with an issue I have had for the past 3 months with attempting to get promoted but not receiving the proper assistance from multiple Non Commissioned Officers within my company and battalion. To briefly explain my issue I have just returned from Kandahar, Afghanistan on ____ 13th ____ and have had enough promotion points for _____, _____, and now _____'s cut-off promotions scores but each time have been told that I have lost my promotable status or my paperwork has been improperly updated by other army personnel. I have already sent part of this issue through your website once, but since seeking your help I have had much more to add and update you and your staff with. I am asking your help to look over the detailed time line that I have provided, as well as the documented E-mails from myself to other leadership. I have also included list of contacts. I hope this information can help you in assisting me in the correction and retro-activation of my promotion from SPC/E4 to SGT/E5, which myself and many other soldiers and NCO's believe I have well deserved. I hope that you can also assist me in being placed back into the Military Police Investigations position that I was in but removed from since an investigation took place.
I give you and your professional staff full authorization and permission to pursue this matter. Thank you in advance for your assistance.

V/R,

SPC _____
13th MP DET, U.S. Army

Enclosures:
Authorization Sheet
Time Line of Events
E-Mail Conversations
Contact List
M9 Pistol Qualification Card, signed by SGT _____

ROBERT E. LATTA
5TH DISTRICT, OHIO

ASSISTANT MAJORITY WHIP

VICE CHAIRMAN
CONGRESSIONAL SPORTSMEN'S CAUCUS

COMMITTEE ON
ENERGY AND COMMERCE
SUBCOMMITTEE ON
COMMUNICATIONS AND TECHNOLOGY

SUBCOMMITTEE ON HEALTH

SUBCOMMITTEE ON
ENVIRONMENT AND THE ECONOMY

Congress of the United States
House of Representatives
Washington, DC 20515-3505

████████ , █

WASHINGTON OFFICE:
1323 LONGWORTH HOUSE OFFICE BUILDING
(202) 225-6405

DISTRICT OFFICES:
1045 NORTH MAIN STREET
SUITE 6
BOWLING GREEN, OH 43402
(419) 354-8700

101 CLINTON STREET
SUITE 1200
DEFIANCE, OH 43512
(419) 782-1996

11 EAST MAIN STREET
NORWALK, OH 44857
(419) 656-0206

MG ████ ████
Chief of Army Legislative Liaison
United States Department of the Army
1600 Army Pentagon, Room 1E416
Washington, DC 20310-1600

Dear General ████████,

    I received the enclosed correspondence from my constituent, SPC ████ ████ of
████, ███, Social Security number ████████. Mr. ████ has contacted me for assistance
regarding his delay in receiving a promotion.

    I would appreciate your review of Mr. ████ documents. Please provide a reply to my
Bowling Green office that addresses his situation. Should you have any questions or require
further information, my staff may be reached by calling (████) ████.

    Thank you for your attention to my inquiry.

Sincerely,

Robert E. Latta
Member of Congress

REL/ts
Enclosures

ROBERT E. LATTA
5TH DISTRICT, OHIO

ASSISTANT MAJORITY WHIP

VICE CHAIRMAN
CONGRESSIONAL SPORTSMEN'S CAUCUS

COMMITTEE ON
ENERGY AND COMMERCE

SUBCOMMITTEE ON
COMMUNICATIONS AND TECHNOLOGY

SUBCOMMITTEE ON HEALTH

SUBCOMMITTEE ON
ENVIRONMENT AND THE ECONOMY

Congress of the United States
House of Representatives
Washington, DC 20515-3505

WASHINGTON OFFICE:
1323 LONGWORTH HOUSE OFFICE BUILDING
(202) 225-6405

DISTRICT OFFICES:
1045 NORTH MAIN STREET
SUITE B
BOWLING GREEN, OH 43402
(419) 354-6700

101 CLINTON STREET
SUITE 1200
DEFIANCE, OH 43512
(419) 782-1996

11 EAST MAIN STREET
NORWALK, OH 44857
(419) 569-0208

SPC

Wahiawa, HI 96786-5494

Dear Specialist ▒,

Thank you for contacting me for assistance. It is my understanding that you believe that you have been unfairly treated in the U.S. Army by being demoted from sergeant and losing Cost of Living Allowance benefits.

In an effort to assist you, I contacted the Department of the Army on your behalf. I requested that they review your situation and provide me with a report that addresses your concerns. You may be assured that I will be in touch with you once I receive the Army's response to my inquiry.

In the interim, please do not hesitate to contact me regarding this or any other issue involving the federal government.

Sincerely,

Robert E. Latta
Member of Congress

REL/al

DEPARTMENT OF THE ARMY
 MILITARY POLICE COMPANY
Schofield Barracks, HI 96857

REPLY TO
ATTENTION OF

APTS-MPB-

MEMORANDUM FOR RECORD

SUBJECT: Military Police Qualification Course results for SPC ▆▆ ▆▆., SSN: ▆▆▆, 13th Military Police Detachment, Schofield Barracks, HI 96857

1. On ▆▆ 2011, the ▆ Military Police Company conducted a 9mm Military Police Qualification Course (MPQC) range. SPC ▆▆ failed to meet the prescribed standard and scored 27 hits out of 50 which is unqualified. On ▆▆ 2011, 1SG ▆▆, ▆Military Police Company First Sergeant and SFC Wogomon, 13th Military Police Detachment First Sergeant inquired if I had verified and signed SPC ▆▆' qualification score card. At no time did I sign and verify his score card that depicted 47 hits out of 50, which would make him qualified as a Sharpshooter.

2. POC for this memorandum is SGT ▆▆ @ ▆▆@us.army.mil or DSN: 655-▆▆.

SGT, USA
Squad Leader

Military Police Qualification Scorecard

Inst		Prone	10	N/A	N/A	N/A
Inst	35M	Prone	10	N/A	N/A	N/A
I	35M	Prone	10	1 min 45 sec		
II	25M	Standing without support (strong hand)	10	1 min 45 sec		
III	25M	Standing with support (left hand)	5	45 sec		
		Standing with support (right hand)	5	45 sec		
IV	15M	Standing without support (strong hand)	5	40 sec		
V	15M	Kneeling with support (left hand)	5	40 sec		
		Kneeling with support (right hand)	5	40 sec		
VI	7M	Crouch	5	12 sec		

Total Rounds 50
Expert 48-50
Sharpshooter 45-47
Marksman 35-44
Unqualified 34 or below

Total NO. Hits 47

Qualification: Sharpshooter

Scorers Signature ▓▓▓▓▓ SGT   Date: ▓▓▓-11

Range OIC Signature ▓▓▓▓   Date: ▓▓▓-72

DA Form 85-R

Forged weapons card

RECORD OF PROCEEDINGS UNDER ARTICLE 15, UCMJ

For use of this form, see AR 27-10, Chapter 3; the proponent agency is TJAG-CL

NAME & RANK	SSN	UNIT & LOCATION	MONTHLY BASE PAY
▓▓▓▓, SPC **Botill** ▓▓▓▓		13th MP Det, 728th MP BN (Rear), Schofield Barracks, Hawaii 96857	$2,230.80

1. I am considering whether you should be punished under Article 15, UCMJ, for the following misconduct: In that you, did, at or near Schofield Barracks, Hawaii, on or about ▓▓▓▓ 2011, with intent to deceive, submit an official record, to wit: DA Form 88-R, Military Police Qualification Scorecard, which record was totally false, and was then known by you to be so false. This is in violation of Article 107, UCMJ.

~~In that you, did, at or near Schofield Barracks, Hawaii, on or about ▓▓▓▓ 2011, with intent to defraud, falsely make in its entirety the signature of SGT ▓▓▓▓ as an endorsement to the weapons qualification card dated ▓▓▓▓ 2011, which said document would, if genuine, apparently operate to the legal harm of another. This is in violation of Article 123, UCMJ.~~ *JH* NG

(SEE CONTINUATION SHEET)

2. You are not required to make any statements, but if you do, they may be used against you in this proceeding or at a trial by court-martial. You have several rights under this Article 15 proceeding. First I want you to understand I have not yet made a decision whether or not you will be punished. I will not impose any punishment unless I am convinced beyond a reasonable doubt that you committed the offense(s). You may ordinarily have an open hearing before me. You may request a person to speak on your behalf. You may present witnesses or other evidence to show why you shouldn't be punished at all (matters of defense) or why punishment should be very light (matters of extenuation and mitigation). I will consider everything you present before deciding whether I will impose punishment or the type and amount of punishment I will impose. If you do not want me to dispose of this report of misconduct under Article 15, you have the right to demand trial by court-martial instead. In deciding what you want to do you have the right to consult with legal counsel located at TDS, Bldg 2027, Schofield Barracks, Mon and Wed at 1430, Fri at 0900. You now have 48 hours to decide what you want to do.

DATE	NAME, RANK, AND ORGANIZATION OF COMMANDER	SIGNATURE
▓▓/11	JARED T. HEPLER, CPT, 13th MP Det	*[signature]*

3. Having been afforded the opportunity to consult with counsel and understanding my rights listed above and on page three of this form, my decisions are as follows: *(Initial appropriate blocks, date, and sign)*

a. ☐ I demand trial by court-martial.
b. ☑ I do not demand trial by court-martial and in the Article 15 proceedings:
   (1) I request the hearing be ☑ Open. ☐ Closed.
   (2) A person to speak in my behalf ☑ Is. ☐ Is not requested.
   (3) Matters in defense, extenuation, and in mitigation:
   ☐ Are not presented. ☐ Are attached. ☑ Will be presented in person.

DATE	NAME AND RANK OF SERVICE MEMBER	SIGNATURE
▓▓ 2011	▓▓▓▓ **Botill**	▓▓▓▓

4a. In a(n) ☑ Open ☐ Closed hearing, having considered all matters presented, I hereby make the following findings:

☐ Guilty of All Specifications.   ☑ Guilty of Some Specifications (line out Not Guilty Specifications).   ☐ Not Guilty of All Specifications (line out all Specifications and sign below).

Based on my findings, I impose the punishments that are officially recorded in Item 6 of this form.

4b. I direct that this DA Form 2627 be filed in the:
☐ Performance section of the OMPF.   ☐ Restricted section of the OMPF.   ☒ NA as Soldier was an E-4 or below at start of

4c. You are advised of your right to appeal to the next superior authority: ( ) within five (5) calendar days.
An appeal made after that time may be rejected as untimely. Punishment is effective immediately unless otherwise stated in Item 6.

DATE	NAME, RANK, AND ORGANIZATION OF COMMANDER	SIGNATURE
▓▓/11	JARED T. HEPLER, CPT, 13th MP Det	*[signature]*

5. *(Initial appropriate block, date, and sign)*
☐ I do not appeal.   ☐ I appeal but do not submit additional matters.   ☐ I appeal and submit additional matters.

DATE	NAME OF SERVICE MEMBER	SIGNATURE
▓▓ 2011	▓▓▓▓ **Botill**	▓▓▓▓

DA FORM 2627 (Test) NOV 04 Page 1

A Thanksgiving Spat

Thanksgiving, in my opinion, is supposed to be a holiday that promotes family unity and strength. A time where loved ones congregate and reflect on what they are most thankful for. Unfortunately, this can also be a time of great duress if a family isn't getting along all that well. Thanksgiving for them is nothing more than a pain staking reminder of the problems they are having. This leads me into my next story about Specialist (SPC) James. SPC James and his wife were in a bad way and their relationship was deteriorating fast.

The word "*divorce*" had already come out of both their mouths several times before that particular day. On Thanksgiving Day, these two start discussing some of the particulars for the divorce and end up getting into quite the heated argument. They yelled back and forth for who knows how long when Jessica finally told James to leave. James didn't take to well to that at all. He told her that he wasn't leaving and their yelling continued. After a couple more minutes of yelling, James agreed to leave. When he attempts to leave, Jessica steps in front of the door and continues her barrage of insults at James. James retaliates back with his own arsenal of insults and the two go back at it with full intensity. Jessica had had enough; she reared back and takes a big swing towards James's face. James parry's his wife's assault and the blow lands on his shoulder instead. Realizing she missed, Jessica takes a few more swings out of anger at her target. After the furry of blows, James does something just as stupid and grabs her forearms and slams her against the wall as he tries to push his way past her and out the front door. This same sequence of events happened a few more times as Jessica continued to position herself in front of the door. ***In every safety brief I have given, Domestic Abuse was always one of the topics that I touched on. "Don't beat your spouse, your kids, your dog, your cat, your hamster . . ." I would tell my Soldiers that if they find themselves in this position where they are trying to walk away or leave and their significant other won't let them, call the MP's or the Police. The minute that you put your hands on the other person, you are just as guilty. It might seem silly to call the Police but it will save your career and keep you out of jail.*** James didn't take this advice. Not only did he not take this advice, he went above and beyond. After a few times of pinning his wife to the wall, James grabs his wife by the face and tries to forcibly kiss her. As she is pushing and fighting him off, he taunts her with *"What, you don't like that?"* James turns and punches the front door and runs out.

Later, Jessica calls the MPs and briefly told them what happened. An MP patrol responded to their residence and Jessica's statement was taken. James drove over to a friend's house to cool down for a while. A couple of hours go by and James decides to go back home. He walks in to find that his wife and son are not there; Jessica had gone out to take advantage of the Black Friday sales. James grabbed a couple of pillows and crashed there on the couch. He awoke to his wife and son coming home but just seeing James infuriated Jessica and they began to fight again. She insisted that he get out of the house and told him she had called the MPs already. James told her that he would get a barracks room in the morning but she wasn't having it, she wanted him out now. Reluctantly, James complied and drove up to one of the shoppette's on Schofield. After he pulled in the parking lot, he called the Schofield Barracks Police Station, told them who he was and asked if he needed to come down and make a statement. The Desk Clerk that answered the phone told James that he *would* indeed need to come in and provide his testimony. Once James arrived at the Police Station and gave his statement, he was arrested. This was his second arrest within a 30 day time frame. Really!! James and his wife were both charged with Domestic Assault. James, however, was also charged with Aggravated Sexual Assault for trying to forcibly kiss his wife. His wife was released on her own recognizance and James was picked up that Saturday by one of the Sergeant's First Class (E-7) from the unit. ***Only a senior ranking member of a unit (E-7 or above) can sign for a Soldier that has been arrested by the MPs.*** SFC Wogomon got James a room within the barracks and the "happy couple" were separated for a mandatory 72 hour period.

The following Monday, I generated a counseling statement and called James to my office. We barred James from reenlistment and, because of the severity of the charges, SFC Wogomon and I recommended to the Battalion Commander that this case be pulled up to his level and give James a Field Grade Article 15. Once he agreed, we generated the necessary paperwork and sent it to the Brigade lawyers who drafted the appropriate documents. The strange part is what happened next.

SPC James, SFC Wogomon and I were waiting at the BC's office waiting for James to receive his second reading . . . but so was Jessica. Awkward!! Jessica had agreed to speak *on her husband's behalf?* SFC Wogomon and I congregate in the BC's office along with the Command Sergeant Major. SPC James knocks three times. "*ENTER!*" the boss says. The door swings open, James' feet find the "X" in front of the BC's desk and he renders a salute . . . *"Sir, SPC James reporting as ordered."* The BC returns his salute and the proceedings begin. James explains to the Battalion Commander what happened that night. James admitted to putting his hands on his wife but swears that he didn't force her to kiss him. After his explanation, Jessica is called into the room. She stood right beside her husband and told the BC that what she wrote *in her sworn statement* didn't actually happen and that James never did force himself on her. She went on to say that she blacked out and imagined something from her past but James didn't do what she initially told the MPs that he did. I couldn't believe it. Seriously!! The thoughts about this woman going through my head at this point . . . are better off not making it to paper.

An Article 15 (applicable to any level) is always "read" twice. The initial reading informs the Soldier of the charges they are being accused of and is advised of their rights during the proceedings. After that, the Soldier is afforded the opportunity to go and seek legal counsel either for free on post or obtain their own private lawyer at no cost to the government. After they consult with legal counsel, the second "reading" is scheduled. During the second reading, the Soldier is read the charges against them again, given an opportunity to defend themselves and/or present mitigating evidence, then judgment is passes and punishment dealt.

After Jessica's testimony, SPC James and Jessica are told to step outside while we all deliberated on what just happened. We went around the room and gave our input and opinion on the matter and what we thought the punishment should be. The BC was not buying it at all; he didn't believe anything SPC James or Jessica had said. With that, James was called back into the BC's office a Specialist/E-4 and walked out a Private First Class/E-3. The Battalion Commander found him guilty on all charges. James was reduced in rank and given extra duty for 30 days effective immediately. James was also subjected to forfeiting $990 a month for two months and restriction to the limits of the Detachment area, dining facility, medical facility and place of worship for 30 days. The forfeiture in pay and restriction were suspended and loomed over the Soldiers head for six months.

It turns out that this particular type of behavior was actually typical of both Jessica and the now PFC James. Jessica used to be an MP herself, which is how she came to meet James in the first place. She was responsible for "showing him the ropes" at the duty station they were assigned to previously. At the time they met, SPC James was married and had conceived a child already with this wife. Jessica and PFC James also have a son, that was two years old at the time of the incident, yet James had only been divorced from his wife for a year . . . you do the math. Apparently, Jessica was showing him more than just the ropes. Jessica decided to get out of the Army due to her pregnancy. ***A female Soldier has the option to get out of her enlistment contract if she becomes pregnant. It is a requirement for Commanders to ensure each pregnant Soldier is counseled and that the Soldier provides written documentation that reflects whether they want to stay in or get out of the Army on a Chapter 8—Pregnancy discharge. If the Soldier elects to take the Chapter 8 discharge, the separation process is very quick and they will be out of the military within a couple of weeks.*** Jessica took the Chapter 8 discharge and was separated from the Army before her leadership knew who the father was. James and Jessica were wed soon after James's divorce was finalized.

After his Article 15 and demotion to PFC, James was rehabilitative moved to another MP company. Unfortunately, I cannot report good things about James. James found himself in the middle of a CID investigation for his part in setting a vehicle on fire. PFC James wasn't the pick of the litter when it came to Soldiers. His work ethic was commendable but the decisions that he made on his off time didn't make sense and were overall stupid. On top of all that happened that Thanksgiving day, this Soldier also had to be counseled for not paying his government credit card; he was arrested for damaging government property when he ran into a pole after being out all night; he was counseled a few times for not being to work on time; a true knucklehead on his off time.

* *The following documents include:*

1. *DA Form 4856—Counselling Form; issued to James*
2. *Excerpt from a DA Form 2823—Sworn statement that was completed by Mrs. James.*

DEVELOPMENTAL COUNSELING FORM
For use of this form, see FM 6-22; the proponent agency is TRADOC.

DATA REQUIRED BY THE PRIVACY ACT OF 1974

PART I - ADMINISTRATIVE DATA

Name (Last, First, MI)	Rank/Grade	Date of Counseling
James	CPL/E4	

Organization	Name and Title of Counselor
13th Military Police Detachment	CPT Jared Hepler, Detachment Commander

PART II - BACKGROUND INFORMATION

Purpose of Counseling: *(Leader states the reason for the counseling, e.g. Performance/Professional or Event-Oriented counseling, and includes the leader's facts and observations prior to the counseling.)*

Event-oriented: Charged with spousal abuse and aggravated sexual assault.

PART III - SUMMARY OF COUNSELING
Complete this section during or immediately subsequent to counseling.

Key Points of Discussion:

On 24NOV11, you were involved in a domestic dispute with your spouse that resulted in both of you being charged with Spousal Abuse. You were additionally charged with Aggravated Sexual Assault when you forced her to kiss you. These actions and behavior are not conducive to good order and discipline and will not be tolerated in this Unit or the military as a whole. Your actions are juvenile, inexcusable and bring discredit upon you. This behavior will stop immediately!

I am counseling you for the conduct noted above. If you fail to comply with my orders, action may be initiated to separate you from the Army under AR 635-200, Chapters 5, 9, 13, or 14. If you are involuntarily separated, you could receive an Honorable discharge, a General, under honorable conditions, discharge, or an Under Other Than Honorable conditions discharge. An Honorable discharge may be awarded under any provision. A General discharge may be awarded for separation UP Chapters 5, 9, 13, and 14. An Under Other Than Honorable conditions discharge may be awarded for separation UP Chapter 14. If you receive an Honorable discharge, you will be qualified for most benefits resulting from military service. An involuntary Honorable discharge, however, will disqualify you from reenlistment for some period of time and may disqualify you from receiving transitional benefits (e.g., commissary, housing, health benefits) and the Montgomery G.I. Bill. If you receive a General discharge, you will be disqualified from reenlisting in the service for some period of time and you will be ineligible for some benefits including the Montgomery G.I. bill. If you receive an Under Other Than Honorable conditions discharge, you will be ineligible for reenlistment and for most benefits including payment for accrued leave, transportation of dependents and household goods to home, transitional benefits and the Montgomery G.I. Bill. You may also face difficulty in obtaining civilian employment, as employers have a low regard for the General and Under Other Than Honorable conditions discharges. Although there are agencies to which you may apply to have the character of your discharge changed, it is unlikely that any such applications will be successful.

OTHER INSTRUCTIONS
This form will be destroyed upon: reassignment *(other than rehabilitative transfers)* , separation at ETS, or upon retirement. For separation requirements and notification of loss of benefits/consequences see local directives and AR 635-200.

STATEMENT OF ███████████ TAKEN AT Schofield Bks DATED 20111125 ███████

B. STATEMENT (Continued)

Q: ████████████████

A: ████████████

Q: Is the ~~fight~~ verbal altercation since the divorce
process ~~started~~ first ?

A: No ████

Q: How often have their been verbal altercations?

A: At least once a day. ████

Q: Were you physicaly touched at any point by your
husband ██████████ ?

A: Yes. ████

Q: How were you touched?

A: ~~When he had me cornered~~ he grabbed my face
and tried to force me to kiss him. ████

Q: Where were you touched?

A: his hands were on my cheeks. ████

Q: How many times did you ask him to stop?

A: Approximately 5 or 6 times. ████

Q: Where in the house were you cornered?

A: In the hallway on the wall inside the front door ████

Q: Did you feel threatened?

A: No. ████

Q: At any time were you in fear of being hurt?

A: Yes. ████

Q: What did your husband ~~do when you said to leave you~~
alone ?

Immorality at its Best

've had a few "bad eggs" throughout my tenure in command but none as rotten as Specialist (SPC) Hanson. Hanson worked at the Fort Shafter, HI Police Station as a traffic accident investigator. Hanson was a liar and an all around bad guy. The next few paragraphs outline only a couple of instances where SPC Hanson's moral compass needed major adjustments

The first incident is about a dog that Hanson stole from another Soldier. Hanson looked online and found a dog for sale on Craigslist. The owner was an infantry Soldier stationed at Schofield who was married with a baby on the way. This soon to be father was attempting to re-home their German Shepherd for the health of their new baby. Unfortunately, this Soldier didn't know who he was dealing with.

Hanson contacted the dog owner. *"I wanna get a surprise for my wife. She's deployed and loves these kinds of dogs. I wanna have it for her when she gets back"* Hanson tells the dog owner. This was the first lie of many that he would tell. *Hanson's wife was not deployed. She wasn't even in the military!!* The Soldier invites Hanson to their house so he can see the dog and play with her a little bit. At the end of the visit, Hanson decides he liked the dog and agrees to take her. The Soldier was asking for a $300 re-homing fee for the dog. Hanson replied *"I don't have the money right now but I can give it to you when I get paid on the 1st."* The Soldier, being a fellow Specialist, knew about tight money situations and sympathized with Hanson predicament. The Soldier agreed to allow Hanson to take the dog home and wait for payment when the 1ˢᵗ of the month rolled around.

Well, the 1ˢᵗ came and went but Hanson did not show up to pay for the dog. The family and Hanson went back and forth via text message inquiring about their fee and their dog. Hanson kept telling them that he would pay but kept pushing his date back further and further. Eventually, the Soldier and his wife told him *"We don't want your money, just give us our dog back"* but Hanson refused. More and more text messages and attempted phone calls had passed between Hanson and this family but no success. Hanson even tried to get them off his back by pretending that he didn't know who they were, that the person they were texting just got the phone number issued to them and asked them to stop texting him.

After repeatedly attempting to get his dog back from Hanson, the Soldier went to the Police Station to file a complaint about Hanson. As he was telling the story to the Desk Clerk behind the counter, the clerk realized they knew who the Soldier was talking about and called SSG Willis. The Soldier didn't know Hanson was an MP nor did he know the person he was talking to behind the counter knew Hanson and was in the same unit. SSG Willis rode up to the Police Station and talked to the Soldier. The Soldier had with him a stack of all the texts messages between him and Hanson. SSG Willis verified Hanson's number from our alert roster and knew that it was indeed Hanson that this Soldier had been conversing with.

SSG Willis brought the issue to SFC Wogomon along with the text messages the Soldier had. SFC Wogomon called Hanson up to his office and confronted him on the issue. *"Where's this guys dog?"* SFC Wogomon asks. *"I don't know what you're talking about. What dog?"*

Hanson replied, as he attempts to finagle and bullshit his way out of the spot he found himself in. *"Don't lie to me."* SFC Wogomon breaks out the text messages and asks again, *"Where is this guy's dog? This is your phone number so tell me where the dog is now."* Hanson finally replies with *"I sold it."* This guy not only stole this dog from a trusting family but then turned around and sold it for a profit.

Unfortunately, Hanson did not commit a crime against the government. Being an asshole and immoral is not a punishable offense. I had no recourse to take. I could not officially order Hanson to give back the dog. The Soldier's mistake was letting Hanson take the dog without paying for it first. Hanson took advantage of the Soldiers mistake and trust and stole this guy's dog. The only thing the Soldier could do is to file a suit against Hanson in Civil Court. I was sympathetic to this guy's case but helpless to lawfully get his dog back.

The second incident takes place in downtown Honolulu at the Fort DeRussey parking lot. This story isn't as f***ed up as the one above but it gives more insight into the nature of this Soldier. It was well into the early Sunday morning hours when all the party goers were finding their way from the clubs or bars back to their cars. Hanson and a younger Soldier, an MP, were doing a walking patrol there in the parking lot when they spotted a car that had all of its passengers inside but the car wasn't moving. This struck them as odd behavior, so the two MPs stroll up to the car to see what was going on. Hanson walks up to the driver side door. The windows in the car were already down so Hanson starts to ask them what they were up to. Hanson is scoping out the interior of the car as the driver was talking and noticed a bunch of rolling papers and empty Spice baggies throughout the car. Hanson asks them all to step out and, with the help of the other MP, detains all of them there on the curb. Hanson searches the vehicle and the detainees and finds more drug paraphernalia on their person.

__Spice is a synthetic drug that produces the same affects as marijuana. This "fake weed" is sold in many smoke shops around the country and is legal to purchase. Spice use in the military, however, is prohibited. Drug testing labs typically do not test for Spice unless the Commander has probable cause and requests it; the test is expensive.__

Hanson must have been in a pretty good mood that day because he doesn't arrest these Soldiers. They give him a sob story about how they are deploying in a couple of weeks. So, Hanson calls up the Desk Sergeant at the Police Station and told him that he wanted to do a courtesy hand over. *__Soldiers that are detained but not arrested can be courteously turned over to their unit. The recipient can't be just anyone however, it must be a senior ranking Soldier within that unit (i.e. the Commander, First Sergeant, Platoon Leader, Platoon Sergeant—E-7 or above).__* The detained Soldiers get in touch with their First Sergeant and pass the phone to Hanson. Hanson briefly explains the situation to the 1SG and gives him a choice, come get them or they will be arrested and taken back to Fort Shafter.

Their 1SG agrees to come get them but he is pissed when he gets there *at 2:30 in the morning.* The 1SG glares at his Soldiers with disdain and is yelling, fussin and cussin the whole time. Hanson releases the Soldiers into their 1SG's custody but then tries to hand the Spice bags to him too. What!? The 1SG, confused, told Hanson *"I'm not taking those. I'm not touching them or putting them in my vehicle."*

The 1SG piled his Soldiers in his SUV and took off. On the ride back to Schofield, the 1SG called his Commander to let him know what had happened and that the MP tried to give him the evidence without any sort of chain of custody paperwork or anything. That also struck that Commander as odd and he passed the information up to his boss and up the chain it went. Once it got to the initial violator's Brigade Commander, that commander made a phone call to our Brigade Commander and asked the WTF question. Now it starts rolling downhill; the Brigade Commander calls the Battalion Commander who in turn calls me. I start trying to figure out the gist of what actually occurred without compromising my authority to adjudicate if I had to. I did, however, ask the Provost Sergeant where the evidence was. *"Hanson cut them up and threw them away"*. Seriously!?!

Although Hanson destroyed the evidence before any case could be built, the investigation that later ensued found that Hanson was not the one entirely at fault. The Desk Sergeant that was working that night was the one who took the fall. The Sergeant was relieved of his duties, removed from the Police Desk and placed into another unit. Hanson was never formally charged for destroying the evidence but reprimanded for his actions.

Hanson made so many choices that bordered and crossed the lines of morality. Hanson was slick and found a way out of each situation that he found himself in but that didn't last long. A few weeks later, Hanson and his wife got into a pretty big argument one night and Hanson beat her up as their baby cried in the other room. Hanson was charged with Domestic Abuse, Assault and Battery and barred from reenlistment. ___If a bar is not lifted within six months, the Soldier will be forced out of the Army.___ Hanson was removed from law enforcement duties all together and placed into another unit where he could be more closely supervised. The bar was lifted, however, and this poor excuse for a Soldier remains in the military to this day.

As a leader, you have to deal with all types of people. Don't let someone's personality and actions change the way you treat them. You must continue to treat them equally. Like it or not, they still belong to you and look to you for legal, moral and ethical leadership.

A Victim with no Common Sense

I t's difficult to stand by and watch someone make a bad decision. Unfortunately, that's exactly what I had to do in this particular case. This story is about a junior female Soldier in my unit named Specialist (SPC) Mendez. Mendez was a key member of my organization; one of the few Soldiers with a specialty job within the unit.

Mendez was married to a younger, former Soldier who was still on the island and they didn't waste any time; Mendez was pregnant with their first child. This story book ending would end up not being so happy.

One night, the happy couple got into a pretty big fight. Mendez was 8 months pregnant at the time. After a while, Mr. Mendez walks out the door without a hint to his destination and leaves SPC Mendez there to stew in her frustration and anger. Mr. Mendez decided to head to a couple of the local bars to drink away his troubles with the wife. A few hours go by and Mr. Mendez decides it's time to head back home. Unfortunately, the alcohol didn't wash away SPC Mendez's troubles; as soon as he walked into the door, she verbally laid into him. Her Spanish verbal assault was not even understandable. Mendez kept asking him where he went, who he had been with but Mr. Mendez was not being very cooperative. Finally, Mendez reached out and tried to take her husband's phone away from him. Mr. Mendez went into a furry!! He pushed her down, got on top of her and proceeded to choke her to the point of near unconsciousness. After he got his point across, he went upstairs and left his pregnant wife laying there on the floor, bruised and scared. SPC Mendez picked herself up and slowly made her way to the hospital. She was not excessively injured but worried about her unborn baby. When she got there, she was examined by one of the nurses but didn't want to report her abuse to the authorities. The baby was fine but the nurse could not, however, honor her request. As soon as Mendez told the nurse what happened, the nurse was obligated to report the incident to the authorities.

The Police were called and responded to the Mendez residence. SPC Mendez called SSG Willis to inform him of what had transpired. SSG Willis drove over to their house; the police were already there and had the husband in handcuffs. The husband was charged with Domestic Abuse and taken down to the Honolulu Police Station. He was soon released but required to adhere to a 72 hour separation period.

Domestic Abuse cases are typically referred to a Case Review Committee or CRC. The CRC is comprised of medical professionals, a chaplain and a Military Police Investigator (MPI). This committee will review the factors in the case and vote on the severity and potential safety risk of the victim. A treatment plan is then determined for both the offender and the victim.

The CRC had imposed individual and couples therapy for both of them. The committee also required the husband to enroll in the Army Substance Abuse Program (ASAP) since alcohol was a contributing factor in the attack on his wife. A social worker was assigned to their case but this didn't help the situation; in fact, it made it worse. Mendez did not get along with her social worker at all. The social worker was not very courteous or cooperative with the couple and made Mendez feel more like the offender, rather than the victim. Mendez and this social worker went at it time and time again. Eventually, the Officer in Charge of the social workers called a meeting to address Mendez's behavior the social worker reported. I met Mendez and her husband at Tripler Army Medical Center for this meeting. The Mendez's, their social worker, the OIC and I all sat down in one of the conference rooms. At this point, I had already had just about enough of the back and forth and childish behavior so I didn't let anyone else say much of anything. I told Mendez that she had to participate in the treatment the medical professionals had recommended but I also told the social worker that her attitude needed to be adjusted.

As time progressed, all seemed to be going smoothly. Both Mendez and her husband were participating in the therapy and the two were developing their relationship in a positive direction. They also were getting along, as best that could be expected, with the social worker.

Well, tragedy struck again a couple months after the choking incident. Once again, they found themselves in the middle of a violent argument. Mendez was holding their baby as the two go at it, then out of know where, Mr. Mendez punches his wife right in the face. She fell to the floor backwards, keeping the baby in front of her. Mr. Mendez walks upstairs to their bedroom and slams the door. Mendez is left beaten, bruised and terrified. Mendez had finally gotten a wakeup call. She called one of the Sergeants that worked in the same office she did and told her what happened. Mendez also asked the Sergeant if she could stay with her until she had an opportunity to file the divorce paperwork. She was still persistent, however, on trying to keep her personal issues private and didn't want the Sergeant to tell anyone else. Fortunately, the Sergeant had common sense and knew that was too big of a secret to keep and called SSG Willis.

The Sergeant went over to the house to help Mendez get some of hers and the baby's things while Mr. Mendez laid upstairs passed out in the bed. Mendez was very adamant about not getting the police involved. The Sergeant pleaded with her to call the police and after a few minutes of coaxing, Mendez finally agreed to call the police and file a report.

The police arrived at the house right before SSG Willis showed up. The police took a statement from Mendez and arrested Mr. Mendez for Assault and Battery. He was taken to the Honolulu Police Station and put in jail. An ambulance was dispatched to the Mendez residence to examine and evaluate Mendez. The EMT's concluded that aside from the bruises and swelling on her face, that there were no signs of head trauma and she was released on the scene.

Mendez informed us that she wanted a divorce from her husband after all that had already happened. Mr. Mendez had no one to bail him out of jail so that's where he sat for almost two weeks pending a trial. Mendez was going to use that time to set her plans into motion to finalize divorce paperwork. We all breathed a sigh of relief to hear this common sense coming from this young victim. Our relief soon turned to disbelief and frustration when we learned Mendez did not follow through with her plan, somehow forgave her husband and let him come back into her life.

The Honolulu Police Department wasn't that forgiving though. Mendez never did file charges against her husband but the State did since Mr. Mendez hit his wife while she was holding their baby. Abuse to a Family Member and Child Endangerment were the charges he was facing and the State wanted these prosecuted. A court date was set for the two of them but that didn't go as planned. Mendez and her husband thought that the proceedings were only going to be a few hours but that transformed into a few days. The judge had decided that he wanted to see this case go to trial, so a new date was set, witnesses were called and a jury was convened to hear the evidence that was presented against Mr. Mendez.

The trial and hearing of testimony lasted about three days. The Sergeant that Mendez called that night had to testify at the hearing as well. During the proceedings, Mendez changed her story completely. With a lack of evidence and the victim, Mendez, recanting her original statement, the jury found Mr. Mendez NOT GUILTY. Afterwards, SFC Wogomon spoke to Mendez and tried to give her some words of wisdom and warned her that next time, and there will more than likely be a next time, it will be much worse. This is a sad situation to see a young family fall into and is difficult to sit back and just be a spectator . . . sad!

A Good Soldier Gone Bad

Hell hath no fury like a woman scorned. That fury is worse when the woman is a crazy, unstable and jealous one. The next few paragraphs tell a tale about young Specialist (SPC) Oliver and how he fell victim to his wife's anger.

SPC Oliver served as a Drug Suppression Team (DST) operative. DST positions are highly sought after jobs throughout the military. These operatives are Narcotics Agents for the government. The DST is a subsection within the Criminal Investigations Division (CID) and is responsible for combating drug use and trafficking on military installations. DST Soldiers report to the CID office each day but sometimes are assigned to another unit for administrative support.

Oliver's work performance was outstanding. His knowledge of the inner workings of the surrounding drug community made him a viable asset to the DST. The Special Agents in Charge of the DST had nothing but positive things to say about his work ethic and effectiveness.

One day, I got a call from the Special Agent in Charge of the DST telling me that SPC Oliver was going to be removed from the DST because of some information they had received. Oliver was not going to be relieved or punished; he was just going to be fired.

Oliver's wife, who had only been on the island for about three weeks, was assigned to one of my sister units within the Battalion. She went to her leadership and told them that her husband, Oliver, had been abusing cough medicine. *Cough Medicine! Seriously!* She didn't stop there; she also called his DST supervisors and told them the same thing.

The DST supervisor confronted another DST peer of Oliver's about the validity of the accusation and Oliver's peer told the supervisor that Oliver sometimes takes cough medicine to help him sleep. That seemed to be all they needed. From their point of view, Oliver was self medicating and using a substance outside its intended use and over the recommended dosage. The accusation with a small hint of truth could have been enough to put all of his cases and convictions in jeopardy. To prevent that, they were going to simply let him go. I didn't quite understand the issue they had; I understand that he wasn't taking it for a cough, but it was a legal medication that can be bought over the counter. I didn't agree with the call but it wasn't mine to make.

What made the situation even worse was that this was done entirely behind the Soldiers back. At the time all the accusations were made and the questions asked, Oliver was attending an Army required 3 week school and had no knowledge of what was going on nor had a chance to defend himself. The DST Special Agent in Charge told me they were going to break the news to him after his course graduation on Saturday and he would be released back to the unit. As I put myself in Oliver's shoes, I felt frustration and anger. All the factors and variables were present to ignite a huge fight and possibly a physical beat down of his wife; she had just cost him one of the best jobs in the Army, all over cough medicine.

I went to her Commander, my peer, and talked with him about what I was afraid might happen and what we could do to mitigate it as best we could. I had already decided that I was going to give Oliver a "no-contact" order for 72 hours and put him up in the barracks. I wanted to give him a cool down period and let the circumstances surrounding the situation set in before he starts asking his wife the WTF questions. Her Commander also agreed that he would give her a "no-contact" order for 72 hours and let the situation settle down a little before they were allowed to talk.

Oliver was looking forward to graduation and getting back to the "real world" and his job. His DST supervisors congratulated him after the graduation ceremony and gave him a ride back to Schofield; they didn't breath a word of what was about to happen. Once back at the office, they had all of his paperwork ready and informed him what his fate would be. Oliver tried to argue his point of view and get them to reverse their decision but his efforts were futile, their minds were already set. His supervisor also relayed my directive to Oliver and informed him that he could have no contact with his wife for 72 hours. SSG Willis got in touch with Oliver later that Saturday and told him where to report that Monday morning. And with that, Oliver was back to being just another MP.

Oliver was moved to another MP unit soon after his release from DST; I didn't have a position for him within the Police Station. As time progressed, Oliver and his wife started talking about divorce. He couldn't forgive her for what she had done. Their home life and relationship deteriorated quickly and Oliver didn't want anything to do with his wife. Eventually, my prediction and fear came to fruition; during one of their fights, Oliver had had enough and beat up his wife. Both of them were swinging at each other but the wife took the brunt of the punishment dealt by Oliver. After the fist fight, Oliver's wife called the police and had Oliver arrested. Oliver spent the night in jail and his leadership had to go get him out the next day. Oliver was given a Company Grade Article 15 by his new Commander and reduced in rank. Oliver's future in the Army is not as bright as it was before. He will more than likely not be allowed to reenlist and separated from service once his contract expires; all because of cough medicine and a vindictive woman.

Not His Spouse

The following story describes the selfish and immoral act of Sergeant (SGT) Hughes. Hughes was newly assigned to my unit when the incident occurred and worked as a Special Reaction Team member. ***SRT is the military equivalent to a civilian SWAT team.*** He wouldn't work there for very long.

This all started when 1SG Eddy, the 1SG of a sister MP Company, comes to my office with one of his Soldiers in tow. 1SG Eddy's demeanor indicates that something's not right. *"Whats the matter"* I ask. He asked me if SGT Hughes was my Soldier. *"Yes . . . whats this about?"* 1SG Eddy informs me that my Soldier, SGT Hughes, slept with his Soldier's wife. The transgressed husband was the one that had walked over with the 1SG. Eddy told me that Hughes and this guys wife had sex at a party in a bathroom. The wife was also a Soldier.

The proper course of action at this point is to issue a "no-contact" order for Hughes and the wife, initiate a Commander's Inquiry into the matter then adjudicate accordingly. I called the husband into the office and told him what the process would be. The catch in this easy decision was that the husband didn't want an investigation done. All he wanted to do was talk to Hughes and give him a piece of his mind. BIG RED FLAG! That was not a good idea what so ever. The husband explained that, although Hughes would be punished for what he did, so would his wife. These two had kids and relied on both paychecks to make ends meet. An investigation would do nothing but draw out and worsen this already painful situation.

I talked to SFC Wogomon about the incident to get his input on the matter. I struggled with the right "way ahead" due to the husband's request. He even provided a memorandum for record stating that he did not want an investigation done. After some discussion and deliberation, I decided against doing the investigation. I know it wasn't the black and white proper answer but I felt it was the best thing for the victim and their family. I did go one step beyond a "no-contact" order, however, and issued Hughes a Military Protective Order for the wife. ***An MPO is the same as a civilian restraining order.*** Hughes was not allowed to have any contact with the wife or come within 1000 feet of her. I set the MPO to expire one year after I issued it. I went and talked to the husband and wife's Commander, my peer, about my course of action but it unnerved him a little that I wasn't going to report it to the Battalion Commander; so he did instead.

The BC decided that she did want to conduct an investigation into the matter despite the husbands plea. He even went to speak with the BC directly but was not able to convince her to back off the investigation.

This was soon out of my hands entirely. Hughes was removed from the SRT and placed into another unit where he could be supervised a little more closely. He received a Field Grade Article 15 from the BC but didn't lose any rank. The husband and wife are still together but are having much difficulty. They are adamant, however, that they want to work it out. More power to them!

My decision to handle this situation outside the normal guidelines was a risk that I deemed acceptable. I decided to err on the side of what I thought was moral versus what the legal guidelines stated. Leaders, use caution when determining how you want to deal with situations. The safest way is always to punish those that violate the Articles found within the Uniform Code of Military Justice (UCMJ) or the law that governs your area. This route is extremely black and white and definitive. Command and the situations you will face are nowhere near black and white but submerged in a deep and complex sea of gray. Take the necessary time to adequately reflect on what you think the balance of legality, morality and ethics is and you will find the *right* answer. Don't be afraid to take some risk but understand why you are taking it.

* *The following documents include:*

1. *The Memo for Record from the husband (victim) that asked me not to take any legal action.*
2. *The Military Protection Order I wrote to keep my Soldier away from his wife and family.*

DEPARTMENT OF THE ARMY
██TH MILITARY POLICE COMPANY
245 REILLY AVENUE BUILDING 765
SCHOFIELD BARRACKS HI 96857-5099

REPLY TO
ATTENTION OF

APTS-MPB-██

5 September 2012

MEMORANDUM FOR RECORD

SUBJECT: Request 15-6 not be initiated

1. I do not request that a 15-6 be initiated on SGT ████████. The only request on my behalf is that a "no contact" order be put in place between SGT ████ and My wife SGT ████ ██.

2. Point of contact for this memorandum is SGT ████████ at ██ ██ ██.

SGT, USA

MILITARY PROTECTIVE ORDER

PRIVACY ACT STATEMENT

1. SERVICE MEMBER				2. PROTECTED PERSON *(Important see NOTE)*			
a. RANK	b. LAST NAME	FIRST NAME	MI	a. RANK	b. LAST NAME	FIRST NAME	MI
SGT				SGT			
c. UNIT				c. UNIT			
13th Military Police Detachment				HHC,			
d. INSTALLATION				d. INSTALLATION			
Schofield Barracks, HI				Fort Shafter, HI			

NOTE: Omit information in Item 2 that, if known to the service member in Item 1, could endanger the protected person.

3. INFORMATION SUPPORTING ISSUANCE OF THIS MILITARY PROTECTIVE ORDER

SGT ▇ and SGT ▇ are pending investigation for committing adultery while attending a party after they both completed ALC. SGT ▇ is married to SGT ▇ from the ▇th MP CO and have two children.

4. THE PROTECTED PERSON HAS ALSO BEEN ISSUED THE FOLLOWING COURT ORDERS:

a. Civil protection order issued *(Date - YYYYMMDD)* _____ , in _____ Court,
_____ County, State of _____

b. Order issued *(Date - YYYYMMDD)* _____ , in _____ Court,
_____ County, State of _____

Property Settlement
Custody and/or Visitation

PREVIOUS EDITION IS OBSOLETE.

Adobe Professional 7.0

5. As a Commanding Officer with jurisdiction over the above-named service member, I find that there is sufficient reason to conclude that the issuance of an order is warranted in the best interest of good order and discipline. It is hereby ordered that *(initial applicable portions)*:

a. The above-named service member is restrained from initiating any contact or communication with the above-named protected person either directly or through a third party. For purposes of this order, the term "communication" includes, but is not limited to, communication in person, or through a third party, via face-to-face contact, telephone, or in writing by letter, data fax, or electronic mail. If the protected person initiates any contact with the service member, the service member must immediately notify me regarding the facts and circumstances surrounding such contact.

b. The above-named service member shall remain at all times and places at least ___1,000___ feet away from the above-named protected person and members of the protected person's family or household including, but not limited to, residences and workplaces. Members of the protected person's family or household include:

SGT ▮▮ and his wife, SGT ▮▮▮▮ and their two children

c. The above-named service member will vacate the military residence shared by the parties located at:

d. Until further notified, the above-named service member will be provided temporary military quarters at:

e. The above-named service member will attend the following counseling:

f. The above-named service member will surrender his/her government weapons custody card at the time of issuance of this order.

g. The above-named service member will dispose of his/her personal firearm(s) that are located or stored on the installation at the time of issuance of this order.

h. Exceptions to this order will be granted only after an advance request is made to me and approved by me.

i. Other specific provisions of this order:

6. DURATION: The terms of this order shall be effective until ▮▮▮▮ 5 SEP 13 _____, unless sooner rescinded, modified, or extended in writing by me.

ENFORCEABILITY: Violation of this order or an applicable civilian protection order shall constitute a violation of Article 90 of the Uniform Code of Military Justice.

a. COMMANDING OFFICER'S SIGNATURE	b. DATE *(YYYYMMDD)*
	20120905

7. I hereby acknowledge receipt of a copy of this order and attest that I understand the terms and conditions it imposes on me.

a. SERVICE MEMBER'S SIGNATURE	b. DATE *(YYYYMMDD)*
	20120905

DISTRIBUTION: Service member   Protected person (Custodial parent of protected child)
                 Service member's local personnel file

The Dishonest Cancer Survivor

This story was a more difficult story to write. It tells a tale about a Sergeant Griffin and her struggle against cancer, her struggles at work and her families fight against the military. SGT Griffin was a corrections officer by trade, working at the Navy Brig on Pearl Harbor as one of the two Army liaisons within the prison. Her job was to manage all of the records for the Army inmates that unfortunately found their way behind those drab and soul breaking walls.

Griffin and her peer were assigned to me soon after one of my sister units deployed to Afghanistan in support of Operation Enduring Freedom. These two corrections Soldiers were put onto my roster for administrative support but I rarely saw them; they reported to the Brig each day for duty. I came to know the Brig Officer In Charge (OIC), Dave, very well and would occasionally drive down to the Brig to visit and see how my Soldiers were doing.

Griffin was an unfortunate victim of cancer. She discovered a lump growing on her neck which turned out to be malignant. The doctors told her it was operable but still didn't give her the best odds. She would have to undergo intense radiation therapy after her surgery to increase her survival chances. Griffin was a wife to another Soldier and a mother of two. It was quite a sad scenario.

This cancer survivor and her family still, unfortunately, found their way onto the pages of this book. After Griffin's surgery, the doctors gave her a few weeks of convalescent leave to recover from her surgery. Griffin was supposed to report back to work on the 22nd of November, but didn't show. Dave and other co-workers from the Brig sent a couple text messages and tried to call but no answer. Finally, one of the Brig supervisors got a text back but it wasn't from Griffin, it was from her husband that said *"if you want information, call her REAL command . . . the Army."* It was evident that Griffin was getting the text messages and phone calls but chose to ignore them.

Dave got a hold of me soon following that conversation to tell me what had happened and the ultimatum they just received. I got a hold of SFC Wogomon and told him what was going on and he called Griffin telling her that she needed to come up to the office. When she arrived, I asked her to explain what was going on and why she didn't go back to work when she was supposed to. She told me that she was convinced that she didn't have to go back to work until after Thanksgiving and was mistaken on the date that was on her leave form. I believed that to be a possibility and an honest mistake so I gave her the benefit of the doubt. I explained that the way her husband went about handling the situation was uncalled for and not tolerated. I was sympathetic to their situation so I let this indiscretion slide. I told her that she could go ahead and have through Thanksgiving off but was to be at work that following Monday. I called Dave and let him know what was going on, asked him to put all of this in a written counseling statement for her file and figured that would be the end of it. I was mistaken.

The next indiscretion took place right after the Christmas break. Griffin and her family took leave and went to the mainland to visit family. On the return back to Oahu, Griffin called Dave and asked for a leave extension because their flight had been cancelled. Dave was very reasonable and tells her *"That's no problem. Just get a letter or some* sort of documentation showing that the flight was cancelled so I can put it with your leave form once you get back." She replied "OK" and told him that she would call him back. When she did call back, she told Dave that "*The airline won't give me any sort of documentation, they don't want to get involved.*" Her comment made Dave's eyebrow rise so he starts asking more questions. "*Ok, well what airline are you using and maybe I can look it up on their website*" he said. "*I don't know, my husband has the tickets*" she quickly fires back. Keep in mind, that these two were in the Los Angeles Airport, together . . . she could have asked right then and there. About an hour later, Griffin called Dave back and said that she would be back to work on time and didn't need an extension. They bought another ticket for almost $1000 so she could get back. "*Why did you do that? I didn't ask you to do that*" Dave told her. Later that day, Dave went and talked to the Brig NCOIC about Griffin and the events that had just transpired. As Dave was telling him the story, the NCOIC interrupted him and said "*Griffin called me earlier and asked if I could help her with her flight arrangements. Her and her husband were late getting to the airport and missed their flight. The next flight they could get on without paying for it was not until tomorrow.*" When Dave heard that Griffin had flat out lied to him, he had had enough. All of his trust, faith and confidence in her ability to do the right thing had vanished and he didn't want her in his Brig any longer.

Griffin continued to withhold information from the Brig and us which did not help mend any sort of professional relationship. One day, Griffin told her Brig supervisors that she had a doctor's appointment that she had to go to at Tripler. Her accommodating leadership there at the Brig was still very flexible with Griffin's prescribed treatment plan and she had led them to believe that this was another routine appointment. It turned out that this particular appointment was actually a pre-scheduled outpatient follow up surgery that would require her to be out on leave for another three days. Dave and the other supervisors at the Brig didn't know until she called and informed them that she wouldn't be coming back to work. Dave was pissed! I called Griffin a few hours later while she was still in the hospital to see how she was doing but didn't get into about how she went about informing her leadership; I didn't think the timing would be appropriate.

Dave had already had enough of Griffin and her husband's actions. He scolded her once she had returned to work and counseled her in writing. Her husband didn't take to well to that and called Dave to complain but his unprofessional remarks fell on deaf ears; Dave banished him from the Brig and didn't allow him to come anywhere close to it or else he would find himself on the other side of a jail cell.

Griffin's cancer had not subsided as much as the doctors had hoped so her time at the Brig was drawing to a close. The Army was relocating her and her family to a new duty station where she could receive advanced treatment for her cancer. I had been monitoring that volatile situation for a while and didn't want any surprises when it came time for her to leave; her award and evaluation still needed to be done and both of those things take time to draft and finalize. I told Dave he was going to have to prepare one for her. They had never seen an Army evaluation before so SFC Wogomon and I had to help them through the process. Griffin had already burned her bridges at the Brig and her mediocre job performance didn't help her situation.

Dave was BRUTAL on her evaluation draft. He showed absolutely no remorse nor leniency when he wrote line after line of negative and derogatory comments. The initial draft that Dave emailed to me was so bad that SFC Wogomon and I actually both laughed and felt sorry for Griffin. I gave it to SFC Wogomon to edit so we could send it back to him. I also asked Wogomon to give some advice and guidance on what should be in the evaluation. *"You have to put the positive things that she did as well"* Wogoman explained. SFC Wogomon actually went down to the Brig and helped Dave write Griffin's evaluation. Although formatted much better, the final copy portrayed Griffin as a very poor quality Soldier.

This was when things really started getting out of control. SGT Griffin had never really been much of the problem; it was her husband that was the instigator and the schemer behind all of his wife's poor decisions. He was outraged at the leadership at the Brig, SFC Wogomon and I. This Sergeant First Class tried conventional and other unconventional methods to try and save his wife's career. They both tried to play the sympathy card but that card had already been played out. Next, her husband verbally attacked the Brigade leadership by posting unprofessional and false comments onto a newspaper website. The statement personally attacked the Brigade Command Sergeant Major which, in turn, caused him to get involved in the situation. Finally, the Griffins took the last step they could take and wrote their Congresswoman . . . Twice.

The Congresswoman's office initiated two separate inquiries into the matter; one on me and one on Dave. Griffin's husband had claimed, on his wife's behalf, that she was sexually harassed, discriminated against and that her chain of command was not supporting her. Dave was a little paranoid because he had never been investigated before, and a Congressional inquiry was a lot to take in for the first time. This, unfortunately, was not my first rodeo and gave Dave some tips on what to have readily available.

Dave was prepared when his senior leaders came to question him. He had all of Griffin's counseling statements printed and ready. The Navy investigators viewed his evidence and took testimony from other Brig personnel and found that Griffin's accusations were unfounded. As far as "no support" from us, SFC Wogomon contacted the doctor that referred Griffin to another treatment facility and got it writing why they were sending her elsewhere. When my bosses read and saw all we had done and that we were paying for the whole thing, they dismissed any notion that we were not supporting this family. This case was closed and the Griffin's were finally moved off island. The Congresswoman's office was satisfied with the report and agreed that the accusations made by the husband were unfounded.

Although the actions of this husband were frustrating and a significant source of contention, I felt sorry for him. His wife was fighting for her life and he was helpless to do anything about it. He was lashing out at anything he could attack and we happened to fit the bill. I wish them the best and hope Griffin's situation and health have improved.

* The next document is an excerpt from the letter that the husband wrote to their Congresswoman. *

From: "Web Forms" <webforms@hhws-www2.house.gov>
Date: 1/18/2012 3:05:35 AM
To: "WebForms, HartzlerMO" <Web-112-MO04@housemail.house.gov>
Subject: IMA MAIL ON CANCER Soldier subjected to discrimination and fired by the
Navy, Army command does nothing to help
<FIRST>██</FIRST>
<MIDDLE></MIDDLE>
<LAST>████████</LAST>
<SUFFIX></SUFFIX>
<ADDR1>████████████████</ADDR1>
<ADDR2></ADDR2>
<CITY>████████</CITY>
<STATE>███</STATE>
<ZIP>█████</ZIP>
<ZIP4>███</ZIP4>
<EMAIL>████████@gmail.com</EMAIL>
<PHONE>Voice████████████</PHONE>
<ISSUE>DEF</ISSUE>
<ISSUE>WEBRN</ISSUE>
<MSG>
CANCER Soldier subjected to discrimination and fired by the Navy, Army command
does nothing to help
Mrs Hartzler,   Griffin
I am ████ ████████ and I am married to ████ ██████. We are both in the Army,
stationed in Hawaii. I emailed you before about my wife's problems with the Navy and
the sexual harassment and discrimination she endured while working there. Well we
found out that she has Stage 3 melanoma cancer. She was fired by the navy with no
written explanation only told to pack out her desk and vacate the premises. This firing
came after her advice as army liaison was disregarded and an Army Prisoners rights
were violated by the Naval command and her notification to them that her cancer had
progressed.. Her Army command was notified three different times about the
harassment and discrimination and did nothing. They are violating Army regulation
when dealing with her counseling, rating and to make matters worse the Army
Commander has sided with the Navy even though they have not shown any proof to her
substandard work performance. She was told since her unit identification code was
different she wasn't a part of this unit. However once fired from the navy job her
detachment SGT has made her drive 20 miles away from the hospital and her
appointments to the detachment orderly room. Even though the detachment has
soldiers at FT Shafter which is two miles away from our house and Tripler Hospital. The
continued problems caused by these individuals are affecting her treatment as the
hospital has elected to send her to the mainland rather than have her stay her in Hawaii
for treatment because of the lack of support she has received from her company and
the Army in general. Please help us. These officers and NCOs are violating her rights
as a Soldier and have caused her to seek therapy because of the Toxic work
environments she has been subjected to.   Thank you, SFC ████ ████████

In Conclusion

eadership is an art, a science and a calling. Those of you that answer this call will be challenged, stressed, frustrated and develop a dislike for your phone. Any leadership position comes with inherent struggles and difficulties but the reward is worth all the negativity. You have an opportunity to impact a life in a positive way, bring peace of mind to your subordinates and create a work environment that makes people WANT to come to work. You have the opportunity to impart your wisdom, guidance and advice to someone that might be going through a hard time in their life. The trust you build with your subordinates will last a life time.

I hope that each story you read got you thinking about how you might handle that particular situation. Would you do the same thing? Would you do something different? Why? Answering these question will help prepare you for stepping into a leadership position.

My solutions are not "cookie-cutter." Each situation that you will face will always be unique from any other situation that anyone else has dealt with. Although the crime/situation and concept might be the same, the variables are always different. Use caution not to blindly apply someone else's solution to your problem. Weigh all the factors, consider all the variables, research other solutions that have been utilized in the past and then determine the legal, moral and ethical course of action.

Finally, understand that leadership is not about you. You are a servant to your subordinates and wouldn't even have a job if it wasn't for them. The decisions that you make have a direct impact on people. They are looking to you, trusting you, to do the right thing, make good decisions and to have their best interests in mind. Your subordinates will pay the consequences for your failure(s). Don't take your responsibilities and duties lightly, embrace them, treat your subordinates with dignity and respect and you will be successful.